How to set up

a

Self-Catering Holiday

Property

2023

Everything you need to know if you are considering running a self-catering holiday property

The 2023 edition

Copyright © 2023 Rob Horlock

All rights reserved.

ISBN: 9798373278720

All rights reserved. You may not copy, distribute, transmit, reproduce or otherwise make available this publication (or any part of it) in any form, or by any means (electronic, digital, optical, mechanical, photocopying, recording or otherwise). Any person who does any unauthorized act in relation to this publication may be liable to criminal prosecution and civil claims for damages.

All recommendations in this book are offered in good faith and the author will not receive any financial benefit.

CONTENTS

Introduction 1

Property or Stocks and Shares? 4

Buy to Let v Furnished Holiday Let 8

Our Experience 15

Furnished Holiday Let – a definition 18

The UK Domestic Tourism Market – some statistics 20

Who stays in a Furnished Holiday let? 25

Planning your venture 28

Financial considerations 31

What type of property should I buy? 38

Who is your Target Market? 46

Should I accept dogs in my Furnished Holiday Let? 48

Electric Vehicles (EVs) 51

Managing your Furnished Holiday Let 62

Holiday Accommodation Accreditation Schemes 66

Rules, Regulations and Safety 70

Fitting out your Furnished Holiday Let 87

Setting up your Administration 99

Setting up your Commercials 110

Building your Support Network 117

Marketing your Furnished Holiday Let 119

Administering your Furnished Holiday Let 144

The Changeover 152

What could possibly go wrong? 165

Nice things about managing a Furnished Holiday Let... 213

Checklist 219

In Conclusion 222

Appendices 223

Introduction

If you are thinking about purchasing this book, or have already bought it, it's fair to assume that you are considering running a self-catering holiday property – officially known as a 'Furnished Holiday Let'. You may already own a holiday cottage or apartment and are thinking about generating some income by letting it out to friends, family or the world in general.

You may have come into an inheritance and you're looking at ways to invest it.

Your current property includes a barn that could be turned into holiday accommodation. You might have land which would be suitable to use for a Shepherd's Hut, or several Shepherd's Huts.

You might have enjoyed a really nice self-catering holiday yourself and thought that owning a holiday cottage could be an opportunity for you.

Or you might own a Buy to Let property and due to the various tax changes over recent years, you're considering changing your property into a Holiday Let.

Covid-19 led to a massive increase in interest for staycations in the UK. At the time, it was safer to stay in the UK to holiday than going abroad (when travelling abroad was allowed). Many people who took a staycation for the first time during Covid-19 will continue to take staycations in the future, either as a main holiday or as a second (or third) holiday. The market for renting a Furnished Holiday Let is growing.

So too is the interest in buying a property to rent out as a Furnished Holiday Let!

Whatever your motives for thinking about renting out a holiday cottage or apartment (or caravan or yurt), there are a host of things to consider before you part with any money.

The aim of this book is to guide you through everything that you need to think about when setting up and running your Furnished Holiday Let business (and yes, it is a business, not a hobby). This book is a shortcut to success. I will tell you the pitfalls to avoid, lessons which we have learnt the hard way and which you can circumvent and boost your profits more quickly.

This book is not a guide to buying a property. There are many good publications that will help you in the purchase of a property, much of which I suspect you already know. This book will help you to consider whether a property has the potential to become a profitable business – most properties can be turned into a Furnished Holiday Let business, not all of them have the potential to be profitable.

HOW TO SET UP AND RUN A SELF-CATERING HOLIDAY PROPERTY

My wife, Karen and I owned a holiday cottage for 15 years. Along the way we made plenty of mistakes, met some lovely people and a (very) few not so charming people. We worked hard to provide a great holiday experience for our guests and our Visitors' Books were full of very complimentary comments.

If you are seriously considering running a Furnished Holiday Let business and want to avoid the elephant traps that can catch out the unwary, this book will help you. It could be the best few pounds you ever spend!

There are number of fairly complex website links in the book. In the Kindle version these links are 'live' (clickable).

I have left them in the paperback version as you may want to follow up some of the useful information provided.

The book is updated annually, to ensure that references remain current. This is the 2023 version.

Property or Stocks and Shares?

At this point you may already own a second property which you are thinking of renting out as a Furnished Holiday Let.

If, though, you are still at the point of weighing up whether to buy another property to rent out you will also be considering the benefits and the risks involved, compared to investing your money elsewhere, primarily in stocks and shares via your SIPP, ISA or other share trading account.

As a quick reminder, **points to consider when investing in stocks and shares are:**

(Note – the following should not be taken as formal financial advice. You should contact a financial advisor for more detailed guidance).

Stocks and Shares

You can invest up to £20,000 annually into an ISA without paying tax on dividend income or investment growth when you sell.

You can invest up to £40,000 annually (or 100% of your income, if this is below £40,000) into your SIPP and the government will add another 20% into your pot (the £40k includes the government top up). There are exceptions to this, though.

You can easily diversify your stocks and shares portfolio to smooth out significant fluctuations in the market.

Stocks and shares are easy to buy and sell.

You will be taxed when you withdraw money from your SIPP but the first 25% is tax free.

You cannot access your pension until you are 55 years old.

The value of stocks and shares can rise and fall, income is not guaranteed.

Points to consider when investing in property are:

Property

Property has been a good investment over past decades. On average, property prices in the UK grew by 5% in the first 20 years of this century. This includes the period of the financial crash, when property prices fell, but soon recovered in most areas.

An increase in value would allow you to release equity to generate cash for other uses.

The property will provide you with an additional source of income.

Property values can go down, in the short term, as well as up. At the time of writing (January 2023) property prices in the UK look set to fall in the short term, mainly due to interest rate rises.

Property has the potential for greater gains than stocks and shares – and greater losses. Consider this example:

Assume you purchase a property for £200,000 and put down a deposit of £50,000, the balance being made up with a mortgage.

If your property increases over time by 10%, its value increases to £220,000.

You put down £50,000 so the increase on your deposit is also £20,000. Your increase is not 10%, it is 40%! Your £50,000 equity becomes £70,000.

Sadly, the maths works the same in the other direction.

If your property loses 10% of its value over time, its value drops to £180,000.

You put down £50,000, so the loss on your deposit is not 10%, it is also 40%! Your £50,000 equity drops to £30,000.

The example above shows the effect of 'gearing' – taking out debt to purchase an asset.

You will be required to pay an additional 3% stamp duty on the purchase of your second and subsequent properties.

If you fall behind on the mortgage payments, the property may be repossessed.

You will have maintenance costs to consider.

Property takes some time to sell, even in a sellers' market, so your capital is tied up for longer than it would be with stocks and shares.

The points above highlight the main pros and cons of investing in stocks and shares and/or property. This is by no means a definitive list. It will though, be a starting point for you to weigh up your options.

If you can afford to invest in both, over the medium to long term, past performance would suggest that you will come out on top. However, as all the financial articles tell us, 'The past performance is no guide to the future performance. An element of Risk is involved, I'm afraid, in any investment which is not guaranteed.

Buy to Let v Furnished Holiday Let

Let's assume that you have decided to buy that second property. Or, you already have another property, but you haven't decided whether to run it as a Furnished Holiday Let or a Buy to Let.

Before we go further, let's take a step back and look at the differences between a Buy to Let property and a Furnished Holiday Let.

Buy to Let

If you buy a property to rent out as a Buy to Let, you will be renting out the property for Long Term Lets. The minimum period will be 6 months, but Tenancy Agreements can run for 12 months or longer.

Buy to Let – considerations:

You have a guaranteed monthly income, whilst the property is rented out.

The tenant is responsible for paying the utility bills and council tax.

There is limited regular contact with the tenants and the property.

However, you may have a tenant that doesn't treat the property as you would expect, and you may have a steep refurbishment bill when your tenant vacates the property.

You may have periods with no tenants, so no monthly income.

Furnished Holiday Let

You had a lovely holiday in a self-catering cottage in Devon. The children enjoyed playing with the new friends that they'd made, and you enjoyed socialising with their parents.

The sun shone, the sea was blue, and the birds sang. Life was wonderful for those two weeks when you escaped from the hamster wheel of work.

With Working from Home becoming a reality for many people, either full time or for part of the week, maybe you can buy that cottage in Devon and work from there some weeks and rent out the cottage when you aren't there.

Perhaps you aren't in a position to move the family to Devon, but you could see yourselves with a cottage of your own where you could escape and relax for some weeks of the year. And to help fund it, you'll rent it out when you're not using it.

This is a dream for many people but it's also reality for a lot more.

Could it be a reality for you?

If you buy your property to rent out as a Furnished Holiday Let, you will be renting out for Short Term Lets. This will generally be for a week or a fortnight, or weekends (especially in the Low season)

Furnished Holiday Let – considerations:

You can charge more per week, particularly in the summer months.

Since Covid 19 appeared, demand for UK holidays has risen and the rental prices have also risen (supply v demand). However, your costs will have increased also (see later), so it isn't all 'jam today'.

You can vary the weekly price depending on the season.

You can reduce your price at short notice if you have a week(s) that needs to be filled.

You (or your agent) will have regular contact with the property when you do the 'changeovers' between guests.

There are tax advantages over a Buy to Let property (see later).

However, you do not have a guaranteed monthly income and you may have weeks that aren't booked. This is to be expected in the Low season but can be financially disastrous if you have too many vacant weeks in the High season.

You will struggle to find a mortgage provider who will be willing to lend on a Furnished Holiday Let.

You are also responsible for paying the utility bills. You will find that some of your guests turn the heating up high (or very high) when they know that they aren't paying the bill. Given the current high price of energy, this is a big consideration. (There is an Economics lesson there somewhere ...)

You also need to manage the 'changeovers' between guests. This can be a lot of work – much more about this later.

Can I turn my Buy to Let property into a Furnished Holiday Let?

If you have an existing Buy to Let property you might be thinking of changing its use and turning it into a Furnished Holiday Let – particularly now you know that there are some tax advantages to doing this!

There is nothing to stop you doing this except:

Your mortgage will have been arranged with the lender on the basis that the property would be run as a Buy to Let, with formal Tenancy Agreements in place.

You will not have this with a Furnished Holiday Let, so you would need to speak to your lender and re-mortgage (more on this later).

Your Buy to Let will probably be unfurnished. In order to operate as a Furnished Holiday Let you will (there's a clue in the title) need to furnish the property, which could be expensive.

Your current tenants will be paying the utility bills. If you move to a Furnished Holiday Let, you will be responsible for paying these (potentially very high) bills.

There is likely to be more work involved in running a Furnished Holiday Let, unless you arrange (and pay for) somebody else to do all the work.

That's a list of points to consider before you jump into changing the use of your current Buy to Let property.

Trumping all of these, though, is the more obvious question, 'Is my property located in an area in which people are likely to want to take their holidays?'

You don't necessarily have to live in a seaside location or in a National Park, but you do need to have a property that is photogenic or near places of interest. If you have a city centre apartment in a 'touristy' city e.g. London (obvs), Chester, Edinburgh, York, Bristol, etc you would find a market for your Furnished Holiday Let, although this would mainly be shorter Lets (weekends, 2-3 days in midweek). You would be likely to attract foreign tourists in this type of location.

A lot of former Buy to Let properties have been converted to Holiday Lets in the past couple of years, mainly due to the favourable tax treatment of the Holiday Let. This has led to some towns having very few properties left for local people to rent, and this has led to some resentment against the Holiday Let owners. You might want to think about this before making your decision to turn your Buy to Let into a Holiday Let.

If your property is on a housing estate, a Furnished Holiday Let is probably not the way forward for you, unless it's on a very 'posh' estate, possibly with a golf course (and then you would almost certainly not be allowed to run your property as a Furnished Holiday Let).

If you are considering buying a property as an investment, you have the choice of going down the Buy to Let route or the Furnished Holiday Let route. Each have their pros and cons, as we've seen.

If you really want to push the boat out, why not buy two properties and run one as a Buy to Let and the other as a Furnished Holiday Let?

For the purposes of the remainder of this book, let's assume that you have decided to run your property as a Furnished Holiday Let.

Our Experience

As I said in the introduction, my wife, Karen, and I owned a Furnished Holiday Let cottage for 15 years. We have recently sold it and it is still being run as a Furnished Holiday Let by the new owners.

The property that we purchased was a two bedroomed Victorian semi-detached cottage in a road called The Custards, in Lyndhurst, which is in the middle of The New Forest in Hampshire. It had previously been owned by an elderly lady who had developed dementia and who had moved into a Care Home.

Like many properties owned by the elderly, the cottage was in a time warp. Floral wallpaper and carpets, a brown toilet downstairs and a bright pink bathroom suite upstairs. (these things are probably about to come back into fashion, of course!).

HOW TO SET UP AND RUN A SELF-CATERING HOLIDAY PROPERTY

Over the next three months we refurbished the property, much of which we did ourselves. We also had a loft conversion (which we didn't do ourselves) giving us a third bedroom.

The cottage didn't have a name and its address was No 13 The Custards, neither of which was likely to help our marketing efforts to encourage potential guests to come and stay in our cottage.

As the cottage was in The Custards, we named the cottage Rhubarb Cottage and quietly dropped the No 13 from the address.

We had our first paying guests four months after we bought the cottage and bookings started to come in. It was an encouraging start.

I will use some of our experiences as examples as we progress through this book. Whilst it will now be tempting for you to go straight to the 'What could possibly go wrong' section, it is probably more beneficial to you to work through the book in chronological order …

Furnished Holiday Let – a definition

Not surprisingly, to qualify as a Furnished Holiday Let, your property must be:

Furnished (obviously)

Available for Holidays

Available for guests to rent (to Let)

That is not all though.

For tax purposes, Furnished Holiday Lets are treated differently to other types of property investments such as Buy to Let. A Furnished Holiday Let is classified as a 'trade', with appropriate tax advantages, providing that it qualifies as follows:

Your property must be available for rent by holidaymakers for a minimum of 210 days (30 weeks) per year.

Your property must actually be rented out by holidaymakers for at least 105 days (15 weeks). Any time spent at the property by your family does not count towards the 105 days total. Neither do discounted holidays for your friends.

During the 'Low' season you might have a longer term rental. You can rent out your property for a period over 31 days to the same person. However, you cannot rent out your property in this way for more than a total of 155 days (22 weeks) per year.

The UK Domestic Tourism Market – some statistics

Let us first look at the size of the tourism market and how it splits down. According to Visit England, £72 billion is spent annually by domestic tourists in England alone. These figures were up to date in 2019, the last year before Covid-19 appeared. In the years since then the statistics have been skewed by lock downs, travel restrictions, etc so these are the latest figures which give us true picture of how the domestic tourism market is broken down. 2023 will be the first year without the 'Covid-19 effect' (we all hope), so I will update these figures next year.

The figures below don't include foreign tourists, who also add another substantial sum to the total.

(Visit England - Great Britain Domestic Overnight Trips Summary - Holiday Purposes – 2019)

Tourism represents about 10% of Britain's GDP (Gross Domestic Product) and supports about 3.8 million jobs (pre Covid-19 estimate).

Where did those tourists stay?

Destination	% of nights
Seaside	40%
City/Large Town	22%
Small Town	16%

| Countryside/Village | 22% |

Whilst the largest individual percentage of nights were spent in seaside locations, a further 60% of nights were spent elsewhere. You can see that you have a fairly blank canvas from the 'physical location of your Furnished Holiday Let property' point of view.

You will find tourists in most places – 'different strokes for different folks' as the famous boxer Muhammed Ali was alleged to have said.

What type of accommodation did they stay in?

Type of Accommodation	% of nights
Hotel/Motel	26%
Guest House/B&B	6%
Caravan/Camping	28%
Self-Catering	23%
Friend's Home, Second Home, Static Caravan, Timeshare, Other	17%

As you can see, almost a quarter of all nights booked by domestic tourists in 2019 were for self-catering properties – Furnished Holiday Lets. This is a large and buoyant market, made even more so by the fear of Covid-19 when travelling abroad, which has led to more 'staycation' bookings.

In addition to domestic bookings, foreign visitors often stay in Furnished Holiday Let accommodation, particularly families.

If you decide to set up a Furnished Holiday Let, you will have plenty of potential bookings to aim for.

What type of people stay in Furnished Holiday Lets?

Lifecycle	% of nights
16-34, unmarried, no children	6%
16-34, married, no children	4%
16-34 with children	10%
35-54 no children	15%
35-54 with children	22%
55+	42%

Bookings for Furnished Holiday Lets come from all ages and stages of life. Younger people will often choose to go abroad rather than holiday at home. When children come along, money is usually tighter, so foreign holidays are more of a luxury. Adults under 34 years old still make up 20% of all nights booked in Furnished Holiday Lets, so it is still a significant market.

As people get older they may (or may not) be more financially stable and can afford to go on holiday more often. A significant number of holiday nights will be spent abroad but a large share of domestic holidays (about 37% of nights booked) will be taken by the 35-54 year olds.

The largest segment is the over 55s, the so called 'Silver Surfers', (I won't use that expression again) who are responsible for 42% of all nights booked by domestic tourists in Furnished Holiday Lets. This is clearly a huge market and one that you would be foolish to ignore.

How long do they stay in Furnished Holiday Lets?

Holiday Length	% of bookings	% of nights
1-3 nights	66%	40%
4+ nights	33%	60%

60% of nights booked in Furnished Holiday Lets are for 4+ nights. These will usually be for one week or, less often, a fortnight. The vast majority of these week+ bookings will be in the school holidays and the high season. These 60% of nights only represent a third of bookings, though.

Two thirds of bookings are for 1 – 3 nights, which represent 40% of all nights booked. There is, therefore, a very large market in 'short stays'. These will usually be long weekends outside of the school holidays and outside of the high season. This is a market that you should definitely not ignore, unless your property is in a location that virtually closes down in the winter.

A high proportion of the people who book these short stays will be people who have taken a main holiday elsewhere (in the UK or abroad) and who are looking for a few days away in the 'off' season. There are many people who take multiple short breaks, so you have an opportunity for repeat business, if your guests like your property and your area. There is also an opportunity to impress your short stay guests, to the extent that they book a return visit for a week, or even a fortnight!

Who stays in a Furnished Holiday let?

When people are planning their holidays, they usually think first about where they'd like to go. Shall we go abroad this year or take a Staycation in the UK? Shall we have a main holiday abroad and a couple of long weekends somewhere in the UK?

Once this is decided, or short-listed, the decision then moves to 'what type of accommodation do we need?' Our holiday planners have a wide choice of options:

- Hotel
- Bed and Breakfast
- Guest House
- Pub
- Hostel
- Self-Catering Holiday Let
- Room in Private House (Airbnb)
- Second Home
- Log Cabin
- Static Caravan
- Shepherd's Hut
- Boat hire – Narrowboat or River Cruiser
- Glamping - pre-erected Tents or Yurts
- Camping on a Campsite
- Wild Camping
- Stay with Relatives
- Etc

HOW TO SET UP AND RUN A SELF-CATERING HOLIDAY PROPERTY

It's a very wide field! If you decide to run a Furnished Holiday Let you have stiff competition, but the statistics tell us that all types of holiday accommodation have a large and viable market.

Why would somebody choose to stay in your Furnished Holiday Let rather than stay in a B&B or on a Campsite?

Each of these types of holiday accommodation have different benefits and some negatives:

Our holiday planners might be on a tight budget, so that could rule out hotels and the more expensive end of the market.

They might have children who need space and less formality so a Furnished Holiday Let or camping might be a favourite option.

They might be dog owners, who would find the choice of accommodation more restricted.

They might be a couple, who prefer to have everything done for them and a hotel would be perfect for them.

They might be a single traveller who just wants to pay for a room, not a whole cottage.

As we have seen in the statistics, each of these types of holiday accommodation will find a market for their business. Who would most likely be attracted to a Furnished Holiday Let?

First and foremost, it will be people who want to look after themselves. They don't want to be restricted by pre-arranged mealtimes, etc and want to be able to come and go as they please.

People who want their own space, without sharing amenities with others

People who want to relax

People who have children that need physical boundaries to keep them safe.

People who have dogs and who need some outside space that is secure.

Etc

In a later chapter we will look at how you define your target market. As you can see from this last section, you have a wide choice of potential guests to aim at.

HOW TO SET UP AND RUN A SELF-CATERING HOLIDAY PROPERTY

Planning your venture

Kirsty and Phil gave their careers a turbo boost when they first fronted the TV property finder show Location, Location, Location. And for good reason. Location is probably the single most important consideration when buying an investment property (or any property).

Kirsty and Phil spend their time finding properties for their TV 'clients' that have some of these attributes:

The least valuable property on the best road.

Close to a railway station.

Within commuting distance of the clients' workplace.

Near family and friends.

Near a support network.

In the catchment area of a good school(s).

Recreational opportunities nearby.

Areas that are 'on the up'.

When you are considering buying a holiday home to rent out, Location, Location, Location is equally important to you – but the reasons will be very different. You are searching for a property that's situated where people will want to go on holiday. They aren't interested in whether or not it's near a railway station (much better if it's a long way away from a busy railway station, unless it's a city centre apartment), neither are they interested in the quality of the schools or the commuting distance to the city centre.

You need to consider things such as:

Where do you like to go on holiday? If the property that you buy for your Furnished Holiday Let is going to be your holiday home as well, you will want it to be located in an area that you like to visit.

Will other people want to take their holidays in this location?

What type of property should you buy?

Is it a seasonal location (near a beach, for example) where your opportunities to rent out the property are limited to a specific time of the year (but you can charge more), or is there the opportunity to rent out the property for holidays throughout the year – The Cotswolds, The Lake District, National Parks and country areas within easy reach of large cities (for long weekends in the 'low' season) are all good bets for all year round bookings.

Are you planning to run the holiday business yourself and manage the cleaning and weekly 'changeovers'? If so, your holiday property needs to be within easy reach of your home.

HOW TO SET UP AND RUN A SELF-CATERING HOLIDAY PROPERTY

Who is your target market? Families, older couples, dog owners, walkers, surfers, stag and hen parties (I'd be careful with that one), etc. All of these will have different needs and you can't satisfy everyone.

We'll look at these in more detail later.

You may also think about buying a holiday home abroad, to rent out for holidays. The same considerations apply but you should seek professional advice from an agency that specialises in this area.

Financial considerations

NOTE: This section is provided as a guide, it is not formal financial advice. You should contact a financial advisor and/or accountant to discuss your individual position and requirements.

Before we go any further, let's review the financial considerations that you need to understand before you jump in feet first and commit to purchasing your potential Furnished Holiday Let.

Funding the Purchase – mortgages

The property that you choose to buy will largely be determined by your budget. Yes, you'd love to own that lovely thatched cottage overlooking the duck pond in the Cotswolds but your budget won't quite stretch to the £1.3 million asking price!

You are highly likely to need a mortgage to purchase your holiday home. This is where life becomes slightly more difficult. Most lenders will not lend against a property that you are planning to let out unless you have formal Tenancy Agreements with your tenants, for a minimum of 6 months. A Buy to Let property falls into this category and most lenders will fund Buy to Let mortgages.

You won't have formal letting agreements with your holidaymakers, who will typically stay in your property for a week or a long weekend.

Your mortgage choices are limited and if you do find a lender, you will need to put in a substantial deposit. 25% would be the minimum, 40% to get a better interest rate on the loan.

A mortgage advisor who specialises in this area can help you to find a suitable mortgage – for a fee, of course.

An alternative funding option, which many people take up, is to re-mortgage your home. If you have substantial equity in your home, this should be relatively easy. It will also be a cheaper way of raising the money.

Flying Freeholds

If you are buying a cottage as your Furnished Holiday Let, the property may well be in a row of terraced cottages. Not everyone can afford a detached cottage standing in its own grounds!

In the past, it was not uncommon for the bedroom of one cottage to be above the front room of the neighbouring cottage. This arrangement is known as a Flying Freehold.

You are very unlikely to be able to find a mortgage lender who will fund your purchase if you have a Flying Freehold. If you do fall in love with a cottage that has a Flying Freehold, you will need to fund it through savings or re-mortgaging your own property. Flying Freeholds are more common than you might expect.

Income Tax

Assuming that you make a profit, you will be required to pay Income Tax. The rate that you pay will depend on any other earnings. Your Furnished Holiday Let profits will be added to other earnings to give you a total on which to pay tax.

At the time of writing (2023), Income Tax in the UK (except Scotland, which has different bands) is applied as follows:

Tax free allowance: £12,570

20% on annual earnings above the PAYE tax threshold and up to an additional £37,700

40% on annual earnings from £37,701 to £150,000

45% on annual earnings above £150,000

Council Tax or Business Rates?

When you purchase your property, it will be registered to pay Council Tax to the local council, unless it is already being managed as a Furnished Holiday Let.

You can continue to pay the Council Tax at the appropriate rate. Some councils are now clamping down on second homes and are applying higher council tax rates on these second homes. Some councils are setting the rate for second homes at 200% - twice the rate of a 'first home'.

However, as your Furnished Holiday Let is a business, you can register to pay Business Rates instead of Council Tax.

The good news is that you may be eligible for Small Business Rates Relief. You will qualify for this if:

You only own one Furnished Holiday Let property.

The Rateable Value of the property is less than £15,000.

If the Rateable Value is less than £12,000 (highly likely) then you will receive 100% Business Rates Relief – that's right, you won't pay any Business Rates at all!

If the Rateable Value is £12,001 to £15,000, the rate of relief will go down gradually from 100% to 0% as the Rateable Value increases.

You will need to contact your local council to find out where you stand on this.

Capital Gains Tax

You haven't even started you Furnished Holiday Let business yet, you probably haven't even purchased the property yet, so why are we thinking about Capital Gains Tax, which only becomes payable when we sell the property?

It is important to be aware at this early stage that Furnished Holiday Let businesses qualify for Entrepreneurs' Relief, providing that you have met the requirements of a Furnished Holiday Let which I covered earlier.

Capital Gains made on a Buy to Let property, or any other second home, will be subject to the standard property Capital Gains Tax rate of 18% for basic tax rate payers and 28% for higher tax rate payers.

Furnished Holiday Lets, though, are considered to be Business Assets and so when you sell the property you have the potential to qualify for Entrepreneurs' Relief. This reduces your Capital Gains Tax liabilities from 18% or 28%, which would be applied on a normal property sale, to 10%. (There is a lifetime upper limit of £10 million pounds on this, which won't worry too many Furnished Holiday Let owners).

In order to qualify for Entrepreneurs' Relief, you must be a sole trader or business partner and you must have owned the Furnished Holiday Let business for at least two years.

This is a very big tax advantage. As ever, though, the Chancellor of the Exchequer can decide to amend the Entrepreneur's Relief at any time, so the rate is not guaranteed (correct as at 2023)

Capital Allowances

Furnished Holiday Let owners are able to claim Capital Allowances for items such as equipment, household fixtures and furniture. This includes the costs of decorating and furnishing your Furnished Holiday Let. You are able to deduct these costs from your pre-tax profits.

All items that you buy in the course of setting up or running your Furnished Holiday Let can be claimed. Capital allowances are available from the date that your business starts trading. You can also claim for purchases that you bought, prior to trading commencing, providing those items were necessary for the business to run.

You are best advised to talk to an accountant about this.

A guide to Capital Allowances can be seen here:

https://www.gov.uk/capital-allowances

What if I don't make a profit?

You may not make a profit from your Furnished Holiday Let every year. You are quite likely to make a loss in your first year. The good news here is that you can offset Furnished Holiday Let losses against future profits from the same property. So, you can carry forward any losses to the following year.

Note that you cannot offset losses on a Furnished Holiday Let against profits that you make from another property or from another income stream.

Set up a separate Bank Account

In order to manage the finances of running your Furnished Holiday Let you should keep all financial transactions separate from other monies. This will require you to set up a new bank account, which should be easy to do through your existing bank. It doesn't need to be a business bank account (unless there are specific benefits to you from having this).

You can then keep a track of incomings and outgoings in your bank account and check them off against the spreadsheet which we will develop in a later section.

What type of property should I buy?

Buying a second home, whether this is solely for personal use, solely for use as a Furnished Holiday Let or a mix of the two, is essentially a property investment. Whether you make money or not will largely depend on what happens to property prices. Yes, you should make a profit running your Furnished Holiday Let, but property prices could go down at the same time, wiping out your profit.

What is your attitude to Risk? The answer to that question will decide whether you go any further with your plans to purchase a holiday home/Furnished Holiday Let or whether you keep your money in a savings account.

Assuming that you have already considered this and agreed with yourself, and your partner, that you are comfortable with taking that risk, there is a vast choice of property types to choose from.

If you are primarily seeking to find a property to rent out as a Furnished Holiday Let, the options are almost limitless.

If money is no object, you could buy a castle, a lighthouse or a remote island with a crofter's cottage.

Those would certainly stand out from the crowd when you advertised your Furnished Holiday Let!

Coming back down to Planet Earth, most of us aren't in that league.

The archetypal holiday home for most of us is a detached cottage with a garden and a nice view of something scenic – the sea or the hills or the lakes. You may well be planning to purchase such a cottage for your own use, whether or not you rent it out to other people.

What you actually buy will depend on two things – what is available on the market in the area(s) that interest you and your budget.

In most peoples' experience, what you would like and what you can afford are not in alignment!

Compromises must be made. Perhaps a semi-detached or terraced cottage is within your price range. Either of these can be excellent choices but you need to be aware that you will be sharing walls. Noise can travel through the wall – both ways – so you will need to be mindful of the neighbours. Your potential guests will need to be mindful of the neighbours too, or 'regular complaint handling' may need to be included in your job description.

If you have searched for somewhere to rent when you go on holiday in the past you will probably have seen a number of modern properties advertised as holiday cottages. These might be modern detached 3 or 4 bedroom houses or bungalows. If these are located in a prime location – a Cornish fishing village, for example, or a

Lake District village with a view to die for – they will almost certainly rent out quite easily.

If they are on a modern housing estate or a suburban road, they will be more difficult to rent out.

Most people are looking for a traditional property with some character to rent for their holidays, so this is what you should aim for. Having said that, most people also expect some 'quality' in their holiday home and maybe some 'premium' features (hot tub anyone?) so you need to think carefully how you fit out the property. Again, this will depend on your target market and how far 'up market' you intend to position your property – more on this later.

You will probably be looking for 'a place in the country'. If, though, your primary aim is to rent out the property, then don't overlook the city centre. Apartments in city centres can be very popular, particularly for weekends and for overseas visitors.

If you look on Airbnb, you will see a lot of holiday properties located on Edinburgh's Golden Mile. They wouldn't be there if they weren't turning a profit.

Having said that, your choice of property should be led by your own tastes and also by your target market for rentals.

Some things to think about:

Should you buy a property that is already being run as a Furnished Holiday Let or should you buy a 'normal' property and change its use? It doesn't really matter either way. If though, you buy an existing Furnished Holiday Let, you will have the benefit of the previous owner's knowledge and you may pick up the list of guests who have stayed previously (but see GDPR later).

You could also negotiate with the seller to leave all the furniture. We purchased Rhubarb Cottage complete with all the furniture. Some of it wasn't worth keeping but some of it was decent quality and was in line with the 'homely cottage feel' that we wanted to create. When we sold Rhubarb Cottage, we also left all the furniture for the buyers. They could do what they want with it – it saved us having to empty the cottage!

Another benefit of buying a property which is already a Furnished Holiday Let is that the neighbours are used to seeing different faces in the property every week. They will be used to the 'comings and goings', which is one less thing for you to have to worry about.

If you are in the fortunate position of being able to buy the detached thatched cottage with roses around the front door, who is going to mow the lawn every week between February and November? Who is going to keep the rest of the garden under control? You will need plenty of time on your hands or (more likely), you will need to find a reliable gardener. Even if you buy a smaller property with a small garden, you still face the same issues, except that the bills won't be quite so high. The windows will need to be cleaned too. If you've pushed the boat out and installed a hot tub, or even a swimming pool, these both need regular maintenance.

Having said all of that, you do need outside space for your guests to enjoy themselves. A South or West facing garden is ideal for sitting out in the afternoons with a glass of something cold, or sunbathing.

When considering a property, you need to ensure that there are no restrictions on renting out the property. If you buy an apartment in what was previously a country mansion, with glorious grounds, you are very unlikely to be able to rent it out, either short term or long term – the deeds will not allow it.

Is it a listed building? If it is, you probably won't be able to knock down that internal wall to make the large kitchen/diner that you've set your heart on.

I mentioned the length of the season earlier. If you buy a property in a seaside location, your main season will run from June to September. You will also have a 'shoulder' season from Easter to June and in October, when bookings will be lower and your weekly rental prices will be lower. Outside of that (apart, perhaps, over Christmas) many of the local cafes, restaurants and attractions will be closed for the winter. Your opportunities to rent out your property will be limited.

There are other areas which are 'all year round' destinations. The New Forest, The Lake District, The Cotswolds and other similar locations and National Parks offer the opportunity to rent out your property all year round.

In the main summer months, you will attract the same type of guests as a seaside location would attract – mainly families. Outside of this, though, you will attract couples, cyclists, walkers, dog owners, etc.

In the winter months, you will have more 'weekend' bookings and fewer full weeks. Nevertheless, the countryside is open all year and it will attract potential guests for your Furnished Holiday Let all year round. Remember the statistics told us that two thirds of bookings in Furnished Holiday Lets are for short stays, most of which will be outside of the main summer season.

The importance of Location has already been emphasised. This is obvious when you are narrowing down your list of possible locations – you will have more takers for a Furnished Holiday Let in Swanage than you will in Swansea (no disrespect to Swansea). Swanage is a holiday resort, Swansea isn't (it's much more than that).

Within this though, there are additional 'Location' considerations. Where will your guests park? If you don't have off street parking, don't buy a property with yellow lines on the road. In fact, if you have got off street parking, yellow lines outside of your Furnished Holiday Let are not ideal – they don't throw off a 'holiday' vibe, do they?

Good neighbours are always important, and this applies as much to your Furnished Holiday Let as it does to your main home. When your guests come on holiday, most of them will be looking for a peaceful break. Noisy children playing in the garden next door is not ideal, neither is a neglected property with rubbish strewn around the garden.

Villages weren't big on planning regulations when they were first developed. You can find a broad assortment of properties along most village roads, some more appealing than others. You might find just the property that you're looking for and fall in love with it at first sight. Don't let your heart completely rule your head though. Look around and see what's going on in the street and surroundings. You don't want to buy your 'perfect' country cottage, only to find that the local farmer's cess pit is behind your garden wall!

At the end of each episode of Location, Location, Location, Kirsty and Phil usually manage to find their TV 'clients' a suitable property and negotiate a successful purchase. Sometimes, they don't find anything suitable, and the voiceover tells us that their clients are still looking for a property in the area. Meanwhile, house prices have risen 5% since they started their search.

Similarly, some episodes end without a successful purchase, but the clients have managed to find a suitable property in the area themselves – but they've paid £50,000 more than the budget that they gave Phil and Kirsty. Cue Phil, shrugging his shoulders 'If you'd given me that budget, I'd have found you a place too!'

Both 'unsuccessful' conclusions to Phil and Kirsty's search should teach us lessons:

If you're looking for a property to buy, don't dither, particularly when the housing market is buoyant.

You'll almost certainly end up paying more than you expected. This is common but remember, if you are going to set up a Furnished Holiday Let you also have the expense of furnishings and other fixtures and fittings which you will need to purchase to comply with the various regulations.

You know all of this already, of course, but before you sign away your life savings, remember that property prices can go down, as well as up. It isn't a one-way street but, over time, your property should prove to be a solid investment – but it's not guaranteed!

HOW TO SET UP AND RUN A SELF-CATERING HOLIDAY PROPERTY

Who is your Target Market?

Our cottage was in The New Forest. So, we needed to target people who come to the forest for their holidays. No Stag or Hen Parties for us then (thank goodness). People who come to the forest like walking, nature, the countryside and many of them are dog owners. The New Forest is perfect for long dog walks.

We defined our target market as:

Older couples with a dog(s)

Middle Class families, with or without children

Other people who didn't fit into those two categories were also welcome, of course, (apart from Hen and Stag Parties ...) but our focus and marketing efforts were targeted at our defined market segments.

Think about who you will target.

If you have, or intend to have, a property on the coast, your target market will undoubtedly include families with children. You might also target surfers, walkers and cyclists.

Do you want to attract Eco conscious guests? In any event you should ensure that your Holiday Let is managed in as Eco friendly a way as possible and make sure that your potential guests know about your efforts to help the planet.

Don't forget that the family market with kids is mainly restricted to the school holiday periods. Outside of these weeks, you will attract older couples, whose children have left home, and retirees. You could also appeal to young couples who do not have children or whose children are below school age.

How far upmarket do you plan to pitch your Furnished Holiday Let? Will you aim for the richest 10% of the population or a more attainable 'Middle Class' demographic?

At Rhubarb Cottage, we aimed for the Top 25% Quartile, compared to our competition, in everything that we did. Top 25% Quality, Top 25% Value, Top 25% Customer Service. If we get those right, then we could justify being Top 25% for Price. As a result of this, most of our guests were middle class.

Think carefully about who is most likely to be attracted to your property – both the area and the size/quality of the property – and target these potential guests.

Should I accept dogs in my Furnished Holiday Let?

Whether or not you allow pets in your property is an important decision that you need to make. For us, in The New Forest, it was not a difficult decision to allow dogs to come on holiday with their owners. Over 60% of our bookings were from dog owners.

Consider this:

> There are 9 million dogs in the UK
>
> About a quarter of UK households have a dog as a pet
>
> About a third of domestic holidaymakers take their dog on holiday with them

Many people wouldn't think of putting their dog into kennels while they go on holiday, they'd much rather take their beloved pet with them. Allowing dogs to stay in your Furnished Holiday Let will undoubtedly increase your booking potential. You can also charge an extra fee for the dog(s) to cover the cost of any additional cleaning. £25 - £30 per dog per week/weekend is the norm.

The number of pet friendly pubs and restaurants has increased in recent years, as these establishments see the benefits of allowing dogs to sit with their owners. The owners wouldn't be there, without their dogs.

This has the knock on effect of increasing bookings in pet friendly holiday properties, of whichever type. If the owners know that they can visit a friendly local pub or restaurant with their dog, they are more likely to book that holiday!

You will almost certainly find that 'bookings with dogs' will increase outside of the main season. Beaches generally restrict where a dog can go in the summer. These restrictions are lifted at other times, which makes life easier for dog owners. Even if your property isn't in a seaside location, if it's within a reasonable drive, your dog owning guests are very likely to go to the beach when they stay in your Furnished Holiday Let.

You should lay down some ground rules for pet owners who bring their dog on holiday. These might include:

Dogs cannot be left alone in your property at any time.

Any significant damage must be paid for.

Any mess must be cleared up.

Dogs should not be allowed on the furniture or beds (although you may be OK with this, in which case insist that your guests provide blankets for their dogs to lie on).

Some guests won't be aware of the need to keep their dogs on a lead around livestock – make sure that they understand this and keep control of their pets.

There may be local rules in force. In The New Forest, for example, ground nesting birds must not be disturbed in the breeding season, from March to July. Dogs must be kept supervised at these times. Your local area may have similar local rules. If so, draw these to the attention of your guests.

You could print out any materials which will help your dog owning guests to understand why they should abide by the rules. An example of this is shown here:

https://www.newforestnpa.gov.uk/app/uploads/2018/03/nfp_nesting_birds06.pdf

It goes without saying that you must have a secure garden if you going to accept pets in your property.

If you allow dogs, though, you will be alienating those people who don't like dogs or who have dog allergies. These people will book their holiday in a property that doesn't allow pets.

On balance, in most locations, I would offer a pet friendly holiday.

Electric Vehicles (EVs)

I'm sure that you're aware that the sale of new petrol and diesel cars and vans will be banned from sale in the UK in 2030. Hybrid vehicles will remain on sale until 2035, providing they are capable of covering a "significant distance" in zero-emission mode.

EV sales have been growing strongly and there are now over 620,000 battery-electric cars on UK roads, a growth of 92% since 2020. In addition, there are a further 440,000 plug-in hybrids (November 2022). Just over 20% of all new car sales in the past year were EVs.

The government has been advised that by 2030, the number of electric vehicles on the UK roads could be around 16 million (usual caveats apply – this is an estimate).

Increasingly, your guests will arrive in an EV, so you could be considering installing an EV charging point at your property.

What are the Pros and Cons of providing an EV charger?

Positives:

- It is convenient for your guests. They do not have to drive around looking for the nearest public charging point. Charging an EV takes some time and being able to charge their vehicle while they are enjoying themselves in your holiday home is

> HOW TO SET UP AND RUN A SELF-CATERING HOLIDAY PROPERTY

much more appealing to your guests than sitting in a fuel station while their car is being charged.
- You are more likely to attract guests who already own an EV. This might increase your occupancy rate in the low season when overall demand is lower and your charging point may tip the balance in your favour rather than a competitor down the road.
- Most holiday booking websites have an 'EV charger' search filter, so you would show up in more searches.
- EV Apps highlight the whereabouts of EV chargers. An EV owner could choose to book your self-catering property, based on the knowledge that you provide a charge point for guests.
- 'Range Anxiety' is a worry for many EV owners (and for non EV owners who are considering purchasing an electric vehicle) so having the knowledge that they can charge their EV at your holiday home is a huge benefit to them (and so they are more likely to book your property). This is particularly true if your holiday property is in a rural area (as many are).
- It reduces the use of a granny lead by your guests (see below).
- It enables you to participate in EV forums, where you can promote your property. https://www.speakev.com/ is a good example

(type 'holiday cottage' into the website's search bar.
- Do your competitors already offer an EV charging point? If this is the case, then you will almost certainly be losing bookings to these competitors from the ever increasing number of EV owners.
- The number of positive reviews that you receive on TripAdvisor, etc is likely to increase as your EV owning guests will have had a hassle free charging experience.
- Eco conscious non EV owners who want to 'do their bit' to help combat climate change may be inclined to book your cottage, even though there is no direct benefit to them. They will see that you are helping the planet too.

Non Positives:
- Energy is very expensive, particularly at the time of writing (February 2023). Providing your guests with the means to charge their EV battery is a cost that you need to consider. Should you provide this as a free service or should you charge your guests? (see below).
- The EV charge point must be in working order. If the charge point is broken, your EV owning guests are very unlikely to be happy guests!
- An unscrupulous person could steal the EV charger
- Your neighbours might use the charge point while the property is empty

- Charging for use of the EV charger might deter some potential guests

Buying an EV charge point

In order to fit an EV charge point you must have:

- Off-street parking
- A Wi-Fi connection or a SIM router (which works at the planned location)

You can buy an EV charge point yourself and arrange for a qualified electrician to fit it. However, installing a charge point is not the same as fitting an extra plug socket in your garage. Specific regulations must be followed.

There are a number of suppliers who will supply and fit an EV charge point at your holiday property. They will carry out the necessary tests and will advise you of the rules and regulations and this is almost certainly a better route to take.

A quick internet search will bring up plenty of potential suppliers. Most of the major energy suppliers offer a 'supply and fit' service. One of the leading suppliers is Octopusenergy - https://octopus.energy/get-an-ev-charger/

The Octopusenergy website has a useful Q&A which will answer some of your questions.

The major energy suppliers also offer variable tariffs, which suit EV charging. The unit price is cheaper during the night hours, when your guests will be using the EV charge point.

Charger Types

Your supplier will advise you on the different options. It is likely that the best option will be a 7.4kW charger. This will be perfectly fine for your guests, who will charge up overnight. A faster charger is not necessary (and will be more expensive).

Tethered or Untethered?

A tethered charge point is one where the cable is attached to your charge point. Your guests will use this cable to attach to their vehicle.

An untethered charge point has no cable attached, so your guest will provide the charging cable and plug into your socket.

Your supplier will advise on which is best for your situation. From the perspective of a holiday cottage, it would be usual to recommend an untethered charge point. Tethered charge points are being targeted by criminals as the cables contain a lot of copper and they're being stolen.

What is a Granny Charger?

You've probably been wondering if your guests can charge their EVs through one of your 3 pin sockets. The answer is yes, they can.

This will usually be accomplished using a granny charger/lead. This consists of a 13amp UK plug, a box containing the charger and a socket which connects to the vehicle.

Many EV and Hybrid owners carry a granny charger as a backup for when they don't have access to a charge point (e.g. when they visit their relatives, such as their granny!)

When used properly and in line with the instructions given by the manufacturer, and as long as they aren't used with unsafe extension leads, granny chargers are perfectly safe to use.

However, they charge the battery very slowly, so are not suitable for day to day use and should only be used in an emergency to put some power back in the battery until a proper EV charge point is available.

Your guests, though, may be more than happy to have a slow charge of their battery using your 'free' electricity ...

How much does it cost to charge an EV?

As you will be painfully aware, electricity is now very much more expensive than it has been.

EVs are all different with different battery capacities and ranges.

Based on a cost of 34p/kWh, the cost of a full charge for the 'average' EV will be about £20. Your guests will probably arrive at your holiday property with not much juice left in the battery, so assume a full charge when they arrive - £20.

They will charge up their battery before they leave – another £20.

Assume they do a few short trips while they are staying at your property – another £10

So, £50, on average.

How will you recoup this expense?

Funding the charge point usage

Let's assume that you have decided to install an EV charge point at your holiday property, for use by your guests. The electricity used by your guests will initially be funded by you. We have estimated about £50 per week's stay. How will you reclaim this cost? There are a number of ways which you can consider:

Make a charge per night/week/visit, as you would if your guests brought a pet with them.

Increase your weekly rate to everyone, to cover the costs of usage by EV drivers. If we assume that 20% of your guests will be EV drivers and they use £50 of electricity, you could increase your weekly rate by £10 to cover your costs.

Do both of the above, but at reduced rates, so that neither the 'charge for having an EV' nor the blanket weekly increase looks too steep.

If you choose to do either of the above options, non EV drivers might well resent paying for a holiday cottage which 'includes' free charging. This would put them off booking your holiday property.

These days there isn't really an expectation to charge up an EV battery for free. EV users, in the main, will expect to pay for the electricity used.

Other options, then:

Install a dedicated meter to monitor usage between changeovers. This would require additional admin as you need to charge your guests retrospectively for the electricity that they used through the charge point.

Leave an Honesty Box in the property and ask guests to leave a payment which they think will cover the cost of the electricity that they use. Of course, some people won't leave anything, but some will be more generous.

Make a charge each time your guest accesses the charge point. This would require you to be able to monitor the usage. This is the simplest option, achieved by installing a charge point with a fob or card that is required to initiate a charge. (The fob/card can be supplied to your guests with the property keys). Sessions can be logged and the EV owner can be charged per kWh at the agreed rate. In most cases, the guests' damage deposit will more than cover the energy used, so the cost can simply be deducted from the damage deposit refund (assuming no damage, of course).

You can discuss these recharge options with your charger provider.

Health and Safety

As stated above, the appropriate rules and regulations must be followed when installing an EV charge point and a suitably qualified person/company must be employed to do this.

The FPA (Fire Protection Association) has produced a useful reference document for this:

[RISCAuthority RC59 Fire safety when charging electric vehicles](#)

Your EV charge point should form part of your property Risk Assessment.

Guests must be provided with clear instructions on how to safely use it.

You should also update your Terms and Conditions to forbid the charging of EV's through windows or using a granny lead (this should be done whether you install a charge point of not).

You must also contact your insurance company and tell them that you are planning to install an EV charging point. Failure to do so may invalidate your insurance.

Summary

EV usage is growing rapidly in the UK and increasing numbers of potential guests are searching for self-catering properties that have an EV charge point.

The costs of installing a charge point are not insignificant, neither is the ongoing cost of the electricity used by your guests. These costs can be recouped in various way and/or used as a marketing tool to increase the appeal of your property vs your competition.

Owners of EVs would appreciate the convenience of having a charge point at their holiday location. They would be more likely to return (all else being equal) and they are more likely to give you positive reviews on TripAdvisor, etc.

An EV charge point gives you another benefit to highlight on your website and helps you to get a higher score on Eco directories.

This is a complex area and must be managed by suitably qualified individuals/companies. The big energy companies – British Gas, EDF, Octopusenergy, etc are a good place to start. These suppliers also offer variable price tariffs, with reduced costs overnight when your guests will be charging their EVs.

Keep it as simple as possible!

Managing your Furnished Holiday Let

When deciding how to run your Furnished Holiday Lettings business, there are two models (or three) for you to choose from:

Outsource everything to an Agency

This is the easiest option and is far less hassle for you. If you take this route, the agency will do just about everything for you. They will market your property, take bookings, ensure that your property complies with current legislation, cover the weekly 'changeovers' and manage any issues which may crop up. Sounds great – why would you not do this? The downside is that the agency will take 20% or more of your turnover (not 20% of your profit). So, if your turnover in the year is £15,000, your agency will charge you £3,000 (+ VAT). This can leave a big hole in your income and if you have a large mortgage, this can be the difference between making a profit and making a loss.

The agency will require you to let out your property through them for a minimum number of weeks per year. If you are thinking of renting out your holiday cottage for a few weeks of the year when you or your family aren't using it, an agency may not take your property onto their books. This is because they will have the overhead of setting up your cottage on their systems and marketing it to potential guests. They will need a minimum number of weeks of rental availability to cover these costs and make a profit. A significant percentage of those weeks will also need to be in the high season, when you might want to use the property for yourself and your family.

The agency may not be very flexible with pricing, particularly in reducing the price to attract late bookings. This may reduce the number of weeks that your property is booked.

Similarly, some agencies will increase the price if the market is strong without discussing this with you. You may not feel comfortable if your regular guests try to make a booking and find that 'you' have increased the price beyond what they might consider to be reasonable.

National companies that offer this service include:

www.holidaycottages.co.uk

www.sykescottages.co.uk

www.originalcottages.co.uk

www.cottages.com

There are also numerous local agencies – if you search for the area that you are interested in, you will find a wide selection of companies who would be only too delighted to help you.

If your property is not within an easy drive from your home, you are most likely to follow this model for your Furnished Holiday Let.

Manage the holiday business yourself

The other model is to do everything yourself, or, at least, 'manage' others to do all the work. In this model, you will be responsible for finding guests, taking bookings, collecting monies, cleaning the property between Lets and managing 'Issues'.

You also have the responsibility to ensure that your Furnished Holiday Let business complies with all legal rules and regulations.

This is a big commitment, particularly managing the changeovers. This will be either a Friday or a Saturday and maybe other days in the week if you rent the property out for a few days rather than a full week. Your departing guests will leave by 10am (or whatever time you set) and your arriving guests will be turning up after 3pm (or whatever time you set). There is a lot to do between 10am and 3pm, particularly now that Covid-19 cleaning protocols have become the standard.

You don't have to do everything yourself, though and you would be strongly advised not to. Best to employ a cleaner who will do most (or all) of the work during the changeover. This will leave you to manage any 'crises' that turn up (see later …)

This is likely to be the model through which you will make the most money from your Furnished Holiday Let, as you will be doing all the work. You deserve to keep more of the money!

This model is the one that we followed as we lived within a few miles of Rhubarb Cottage and it was easy for us to travel to the cottage when required.

A hybrid model

There is also a third model which you could employ.

If you know someone that is trustworthy, or you can find such a person through recommendations, you could leave the day to day running of the property, and the changeover between guests, to them.

You would still be responsible for finding the guests and managing the bookings but you wouldn't need to visit the property so frequently.

This hybrid model would work whether your Furnished Holiday Let is situated close to your home or 100 miles away, or more.

Holiday Accommodation Accreditation Schemes

All types of holiday accommodation in the UK are classified under some form of 'star' system. These vary slightly in England, Wales, Scotland and Northern Ireland but the same principles apply.

The 'Visit England' scheme is the main national quality rating scheme in England. There are other local schemes which you could join instead.

You don't have to join an accreditation scheme. If you choose not to join one, so your Furnished Holiday Let effectively has 0 stars, what messages does that send to your potential guests? I'll leave that with you.

Whichever rating scheme you choose to join, if any, you will pay an annual fee. Every year, your Furnished Holiday Let will be inspected and it will be rated against a standard, to ensure consistency across all properties within the sector. You will be awarded a star rating, from 1 star to 5 stars. (Local schemes may not use stars, our local scheme uses acorns, but the principle is the same – the higher the number, the better)

The majority of Furnished Holiday Lets are rated at 3 stars or 4 stars. If you are aiming at the top end of the market, you will need to aim for a 5 star rating.

The inspection, and the rating that your Furnished Holiday Let receives, is not only based on hygiene and the way that you manage the property. Each rating level has a list of furniture and fittings that your Furnished Holiday Let must have. For example, Rhubarb Cottage was rated at 4 stars. In order to qualify for this rating, we had to provide (amongst a lot of other things) a full size freezer. We didn't have room in the kitchen, so we put it in the small summerhouse in the garden. Never mind that hardly anyone used the freezer, we had to provide it to retain out 4 star rating.

Since then, in order to qualify for a 4 star rating you must provide, amongst many other things, a TV with a 43" screen or larger and a coffee machine (not just a coffee filter and/or instant coffee sachets).

If you are aiming for 5 stars, amongst other things, you will be required to completely redecorate the property every year – that's a lot of work!

In addition to the main scheme, there are other, more focused schemes. Visit England has a scheme which focuses on Cyclists. In order to qualify for this accreditation, you will need to provide a number of additional items and services such as a puncture repair outfit and secure storage. A similar scheme exists for Walkers.

If you have a suitable property, you could specialise in providing holiday accommodation for people with disabilities. This is a specialist area and you may need to make some structural alterations to your property. You will certainly need to provide a downstairs bathroom and bedroom, so a bungalow would be suitable.

Wheelchair access is required, so you would need a ramp up to your front door if you have steps. Your doors may not be wide enough – this will be a common feature in older properties.

Providing holiday accommodation for disabled guests can be extremely rewarding but your Furnished Holiday Let must be properly set up for this market.

Another scheme that is very popular is the Green scheme. Belonging to the Green scheme shows your guests that you care about the environment. The qualification requirements for this scheme vary, depending on the type of property. A property with a garden would be expected to have a compost bin, for example, which wouldn't be appropriate for a property with no garden.

Whatever type of property you have, you will be expected to recycle everything that you can. This will be dictated by the local council. Each council has its own recycling rules – what can be recycled in one area may not be recycled in another area. It will all depend on the local recycling infrastructure. This is particularly true of plastics. Although your soup tubs and yoghurt pots have a recycling label on them, your local council may not be able to process them. It's important to know what can and can't be recycled in your area and make your guests aware of this.

The recycling notice that we used at Rhubarb Cottage can be seen in Appendix 1.

You can find out about the Visit England Quality schemes here:

https://www.visitenglandassessmentservices.com/

Similar schemes are available in Scotland, Wales and Northern Ireland

Rules, Regulations and Safety

As you would expect, running a Furnished Holiday Let involves a number of rules and regulations. You must ensure that you are aware of all of these and that you are compliant.

Furnished Holiday Let Insurance including Public Liability Insurance

Specialist Furnished Holiday Let insurance policies are available and you must ensure that you are adequately covered. As well as buildings and content cover, this must also include public liability insurance.

This is a niche insurance product and providers who specialise in Furnished Holiday Let insurance include:

Schofields: www.schofields.ltd.uk

Boshers: www.boshers.co.uk

Following Covid-19, you must check carefully to see if your insurance covers you against loss of income due to a pandemic.

Fire Regulations

If you have any type of accommodation that involves paying guests, fire safety law will apply to you. You will need to carry out a Fire Risk Assessment, to identify all of the potential areas of concern. This will cover:

- Identifying the fire hazards

- Identifying people at risk

- Evaluate, remove, reduce and protect from risk

- Records, plan, inform, instruct and train

- Regular review

An example of a Fire Risk Assessment for a Furnished Holiday Let can be seen at Appendix 2

You can find full details here:

https://www.gov.uk/workplace-fire-safety-your-responsibilities

Fire Safety equipment

The Furniture and Furnishings (Fire Safety) Regulations 1988 are UK law and are designed to ensure that upholstery components and composites used for furniture supplied in the UK meet specified ignition resistance levels and are suitably labelled. When you buy new furniture or furnishings, these will be fire retardant and comply with this legislation. However, any antique or 'pre-owned' furnishings may not comply. You need to check this before you include any older furnishings in your Furnished Holiday Let.

Further details can be viewed here:

https://www.firesafe.org.uk/furniture-and-furnishings-fire-safety-regulations-19881989-and-1993/

You also need to provide a Fire Extinguisher and a Fire Blanket. These must be checked annually. Ideally, you should have a fire extinguisher on each floor and a fire blanket in the kitchen.

A very useful leaflet on fire safety can be seen here:

https://www.dsfire.gov.uk/YourSafety/SafetyAtWorkandotherplaces/Documents/documents/DS2018-2554Self-cateringHolidayLets.pdf

Smoke and CO Detectors

Since 1st October 2015, owners of Furnished Holiday Lets have been required to have at least one smoke alarm installed on every storey of their property. This must be connected to the mains electricity supply, not just a cheap battery alarm.

A carbon monoxide (CO) detector must also be sited in any room containing a solid fuel burning appliance (eg a coal fire, wood burning stove). These have a lifetime of anywhere between 5 to 7 years, but it is important to check the lifetime of your specific product. Batteries must also be regularly checked.

The person responsible must make sure that these alarms are in working order at each changeover. That's probably you ...

Access Statement

An access statement is designed to highlight whether or not your property is suitable for people who have disabilities. The best way to write this is to walk through your property, starting outside the front door, and moving from room to room. Point out any steps and narrow passages or doorways. Include any measures that you have taken to make your property more inclusive. A ramp outside of the front door, perhaps. Grab handles in the toilet, passages and bathroom. Highlight a downstairs bathroom or bedroom. At Rhubarb Cottage, we included a photograph of each point that we included in our access statement. This is not essential but makes everything more obvious.

You should have an access statement whether or not you expect anyone with disabilities to stay in your Furnished Holiday Let.

A copy of an Access Statement can be seen at Appendix 3

Landlord Gas Safety Certificate

Every year you must have your gas heating system and any gas appliances checked by a qualified gas engineer. They will issue you with the Landlord Gas Safety Certificate (also known by its old name of CP12) and you should include a copy of this in the pack that you leave in the property.

A copy of a Landlord Gas Safety Certificate can be seen in Appendix 4

Energy Performance Certificate (EPC)

All properties for sale or rent in the UK must now have an Energy Performance Certificate (EPC). Apart from being a legal document, the EPC also acts as a proxy for the quality of your accommodation.

An EPC is a certificate that shows the energy efficiency of a property. The EPC rating runs from A (best) to G (worst). In general, newer properties have a higher EPC rating and older properties have a lower EPC rating. Also, in general, properties with a higher EPC rating are cheaper to run than properties with a lower EPC rating. They will also emit less carbon dioxide.

The EPC provides information on how much energy the property uses, how costly it'll be to run its heating, hot water and lighting, and a measure of the likely level of carbon dioxide emissions.

Here is an example of the EPC graph for a property that has been rated at Band D, with a potential to move to Band B:

See how to improve this property's energy performance.

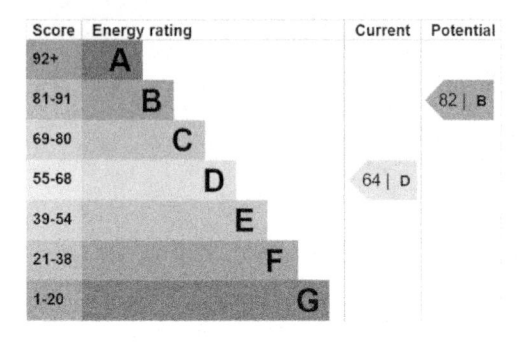

Score	Energy rating	Current	Potential
92+	A		
81-91	B		82 | B
69-80	C		
55-68	D	64 | D	
39-54	E		
21-38	F		
1-20	G		

The graph shows this property's current and potential energy efficiency.

Properties are given a rating from A (most efficient) to G (least efficient).

The recommendations to move from Band D to Band B shown on the EPC are as follows:

Current EPC Rating: Band D

How to improve this property's energy performance

Potential energy rating

B

Making any of the recommended changes will improve this property's energy efficiency.

If you make all of the recommended changes, this will improve the property's energy rating and score from D (64) to B (82).

Recommendation 1: Cavity wall insulation

Cavity wall insulation

Typical installation cost £500 - £1,500

Typical yearly saving £108

Potential rating after carrying out recommendation 1 68 | D

Recommendation 2: Floor insulation (solid floor)

Floor insulation (solid floor)

Typical installation cost £4,000 - £6,000

Typical yearly saving £41

Potential rating after carrying out recommendations 1 and 2 70 | C

Recommendation 3: Heating controls (thermostatic radiator valves)

Heating controls (TRVs)

Typical installation cost £350 - £450

Typical yearly saving £29

Potential rating after carrying out recommendations 1 to 3 71 | C

Recommendation 4: Solar water heating

Solar water heating

Typical installation cost £4,000 - £6,000

Typical yearly saving £42

Potential rating after carrying out recommendations 1 to 4 73 | C

Recommendation 5: Solar photovoltaic panels, 2.5 kWp

Solar photovoltaic panels

HOW TO SET UP AND RUN A SELF-CATERING HOLIDAY PROPERTY

Typical installation cost £3,500 - £5,500

Typical yearly saving £364

Potential rating after carrying out recommendations 1 to 5 82 | B

You can see that some of these recommendations have a very long payback period, so are unlikely to be implemented.

Since April 2020, if you are renting out your property to a long-term tenant, your property must have a rating of at least E.

If you are renting your property out as a Furnished Holiday Let there is no legal requirement to ensure that your property has an EPC rating of E or above. However, if you are seeking to give your guests a great holiday experience anything below a D rating is unlikely to be good enough. Your guests might complain that your property is cold or draughty. Does the Band E/F/G property have single glazing and little of no insulation? Perhaps the boiler is old and unreliable (and expensive to run).

Apart from the obvious need to reduce carbon dioxide emissions, you have a more immediate and pressing need to ensure that your guests enjoy their holiday. If there are simple energy efficiency measures that you can carry out such as draught proofing, double glazing, hot water cylinder insulation and loft insulation you should invest in having these done. They will reduce the running costs of your Furnished Holiday Let (remember, you are paying those expensive energy bills!) and make your guests more comfortable. You'll also be doing your bit for the planet by reducing the carbon dioxide emissions of the property.

If you buy a 'doer – upper' property to run as a Furnished Holiday Let the initial energy survey could well show that the property would have a very low grading. You probably wouldn't have the energy survey carried out until you had completed your renovations, by which time your insulation, double/triple glazing, low energy lighting, new condensing boiler, draught proofing (and perhaps, solar panels) would see you comfortably into a C grading.

There are exemptions to the requirement to reach Band E. If you are running a Furnished Holiday Let you don't need to worry about this. However, even though there is no legal requirement for your property to reach Band E, you shouldn't be thinking about this as such a property would not be good enough to rent out for holidays.

Details of the exemptions can be seen here:

https://www.gov.uk/guidance/domestic-private-rented-property-minimum-energy-efficiency-standard-landlord-guidance

If you look at the link above, at the bottom of the page you will read the following:

Government has committed to look at a long-term trajectory to improve the energy performance standards of privately rented homes in England and Wales, with the aim

for as many of them as possible to be upgraded to EPC Band C by 2030, where practical, cost-effective and affordable.

By 2030 it is very likely that a minimum EPC efficiency grading will apply to Furnished Holiday Let as well as long-term tenancies. This is not something that you should ignore.

If your property doesn't have a current EPC, you will need find an Energy Assessor, who will carry out an energy survey. If you need an Energy Assessor, you can find one here:

https://getting-new-energy-certificate.digital.communities.gov.uk/

During the survey, the assessor will evaluate measures such as loft insulation, boilers, lighting, radiators and double glazing to test the property's overall energy efficiency.

You will need to give the assessor access to all of the rooms in the property so that they can carry out their measurements and take photos to determine the energy rating. The time to do the survey will depend on the size of the property but it's likely to be 1-2 hours for most properties.

The EPC costs from £60 to over £100 depending on the area and the assessor. It's worth getting more than one quote for the job.

The EPC is valid for 10 years. During this time, the EPC can be updated to include any energy efficiency improvements that you carry out.

Although you aren't legally required to in a Furnished Holiday Let, it's good practice to display your EPC in your property. You should also keep another copy in your 'Furnished Holiday Let documents' folder. You can access EPCs in E&W here:

https://find-energy-certificate.digital.communities.gov.uk/

The government sometimes runs schemes to part fund energy efficiency improvements. These schemes have always started with the best of intentions but have usually faltered, for various reasons. If you see such a scheme, you may well qualify for some financial assistance, so don't think that 'I won't qualify'. You might be surprised!

Electrical Installation Condition Report (EICR)

In addition to the Gas Safety Certificate detailed above, landlords now need to obtain an Electrical Installation Condition Report (EICR).

Faulty appliances and wiring are the cause of more than one in 10 house fires in the UK (Home Office fire statistics 2019-2020).

In June 2020, new regulations were introduced that oblige all landlords to have each of their rental properties inspected every 5 years. This applies to both 'Buy to Let' and Furnished Holiday Lets.

This inspection must be carried out by a qualified electrician, who will provide the EICR. This shows that all electrical installations in a property – wiring, plug sockets and fuse boxes – are safe to use and in good working order. The EICR also highlights the checks made during the inspection, and any improvements that the landlord needs to make.

You must keep a copy of the EICR as evidence of the inspection, and to give to the inspector when you next need to have the house checked. Tip: Make a note in your electronic calendar for 4 years 9 months in the future, to remind you to arrange the 5 year inspection.

Your local authority may wish to see evidence that you have an EICR. You must give them with a copy within 7 days of receiving the request.

If the inspector finds that work needs to be carried out, the EICR will be issued with the proviso that the work required is completed within 28 days of the inspection.

Once the work has been completed, you will need to send written confirmation to your local authority within 28 days of finishing the work.

The cost of an EICR will vary, depending on the number of electrical installations that need to be checked. Prices start at around £120.

Local authorities can fine landlords up to £30,000 if they don't follow the rules so, apart from the very important safety aspect, there is a very significant financial penalty for non-compliance!

PAT tests

Portable Appliance Testing (PAT) testing legislation was put into effect to ensure that all companies conform to the Health and Safety at Work Act of 1974, Electricity at Work Regulations of 1989, Provision and Use of Work Equipment regulations of 1998 and the Management of Health and Safety at Work regulations of 1999.

In your case PAT Testing relates to the portable electrical equipment that you have in your Furnished Holiday Let. This will include kitchen appliances, TVs, speakers, bedside lights, etc. Testing these items is <u>not a legal requirement</u>, though it makes sense to check these items regularly and replace them when required.

Portable Appliances are <u>not</u> covered in the EICR above.

Details can be seen at this link:
https://www.hse.gov.uk/pubns/indg236.htm

Employment Law

You may or may not employ staff to help you to run your Furnished Holiday Let business. If you own more than one property, you will almost certainly have to employ some part time help.

Employment Law is beyond the scope of this book but is something that you must take seriously and understand your responsibilities. A starting point can be found here:

https://www.gov.uk/browse/employing-people/contracts

Data Protection (GDPR)

GDPR (the General Data Protection Regulation) came into force in May 2018. The updated regulations were designed to supersede the Data Protection Act (DPA) 1998 and bring the regulations up to date in a world of data overload and the internet.

As the owner of a Furnished Holiday Let, you may well be thinking that this doesn't apply to little old you. Predictably, I'm afraid it does.

If you keep any information on your guests, even just their email address, then you need to think about GDPR – and comply with the regulations.

GDPR applies to the 'processing of personal data', for any business purpose, regardless of the size of the business. So, what is Personal Data?

Personal data is any information that relates to an identifiable individual. So, name, phone number or email address, to more personal information such as their sexual orientation or whether they are disabled. It is important to note that personal information also includes images, including CCTV recordings. As a general rule, if it is possible to identify an individual directly from the information you process, then that information is personal data.

What is 'processing'?

Processing of personal data covers anything you do with collecting, storing, organising and using that data through to deleting it.

Most owners of Furnished Holiday Lets will communicate with their guests through email. If you are going to hold information on your guests for any purpose other than handling their current booking (for example, to send them marketing material in future), then you need to obtain their consent for you to contact them.

If you have a list of guests who have stayed with you in the past, you are not allowed to send them a marketing mailing unless they have 'opted in'. This why you are usually asked to 'tick a box' when you register with a company online.

If they have opted in, then you can send them your mailings and contact them about future promotions. If they have not opted in, you cannot contact them with random marketing messages.

You should also regularly review your customer data, including (especially?) emails that contain personal information and delete them when they are no longer required for the current transaction.

See the later section on Mailing Lists, which relates to GDPR.

Further details can be found at the link here:

https://www.visitbritain.org/business-advice/registration-and-data-protection

The Pink Book is the 'go to' book for legal requirements within the tourist accommodation sector in Britain. You will find details here:

https://www.visitbritain.org/business-advice/know-your-legal-obligations

Fitting out your Furnished Holiday Let

Fitting out your property

By now, you have purchased your property, identified your target market and decided whether you are going to manage it through an agency or do it all yourself (or something in between).

Whichever model you choose to manage your Furnished Holiday Let, you will need to get everything set up in the first place. You should take some time to plan this, rather than jumping in with the paintbrush and covering all the walls with 'Timeless'.

You may have purchased an older property that needs to be knocked into shape or you may have a property that doesn't need any structural alterations but will quite possibly need a new kitchen and bathroom. Remember that any building works may require Planning Permission and/or Building Regulations.

To a degree, your target market will influence how you furnish and decorate your property. If you're going upmarket, then your kitchen fitments and bathroom furniture need to be high end. If you're aiming for the middle market, your fittings still need to be quality, but not quite so expensive.

Kitchen fittings such as the oven, hob and microwave can be very slick, with pre-programmed settings and 'touch' controls. These look great (and are great) but you will have different people using them every week. Your pre-programmed controls will be over-ridden by your guests who haven't read the instructions (90% never read the instructions) and just pressed random buttons. My strong advice here is to buy good quality but simple fittings. A microwave with a knob that turns to set the timer, rather than eight touch buttons which have no obvious function. Similarly, with the hob and oven – simple controls save a lot of anguish, both for your guests and you. If you've fitted an Induction Hob, tell your guests. Many of them won't have used one of these before and will be surprised how quickly a saucepan of vegetables boils and, perhaps, may wonder why the hob doesn't get hot!

Remember that you are furnishing a Furnished Holiday Let not your home. Whilst your personal taste may influence this, your first consideration must be practicality. You (or your agency staff) will need to clean the property between Lets. Hygiene has always been very important, but it is even more so now, since Covid-19 made its appearance.

'Plan for the worst and expect the best' is sound advice. Assume that children's sticky fingers will touch everything. That might direct your thinking over the type of furniture that you provide. Similarly, some colours deal with stains better than others, particularly on carpets! Mattress protectors do what they say when one of the children 'has an accident'.

You will also need to purchase bedding, towels, etc. At Rhubarb Cottage we had three sets of everything. One set on the beds, one set in the wash and one spare set. One thing to be mindful of here is allergies. You may be surprised how many people are allergic to feathers or down. If you are in the 5 star category you will probably want to provide duck down quilts and Hungarian goose down pillows. That's fine until someone with an allergy turns up. If you provide down filled bedding, I suggest you ask about any allergies at the time of booking. If you know that your guest(s) is allergic to down, you can provide synthetic filled bedding for them. At Rhubarb Cottage we provided synthetic bedding on all of the beds and we only had one complaint in the 15 years that we had the cottage. That person would have preferred down bedding.

Your guests will expect a good make up mirror in the bedrooms and bathroom. Similarly, you should provide a hairdryer in each bedroom. The makeup mirror should also be illuminated. If you don't have an illuminated mirror, place a table lamp on the dressing table near the makeup mirror.

People of all ages and demographic like to (expect to?) luxuriate on holiday. Think of the things that you like when you are on holiday. A power shower always goes down well, as does a log burner (buy a multi-fuel version, which burns clean-burning coal as well as wood). This leads on to the 'should we provide a hot tub?' decision. Everyone loves a hot tub but from your point of view, they are very expensive to run and maintain and they are time consuming to check during the limited time that you have during the changeover between guests. A thought: Although the water in the hot tub will be chemically balanced (or should be) and sanitised, you don't know who has been in the hot tub before you, or what they did ... (I'll leave that with you...)

The same question applies to a BBQ. Should you provide a BBQ? When we first had Rhubarb Cottage, we supplied a BBQ – a decent one, not a disposable one. This was ignored by most guests, used by some. When it was used, it was very rarely left clean. When it was left clean, the used coals were left for disposal. This is all time consuming and when you are up against the clock, it's not ideal.

After a while we took away the BBQ. Nobody ever complained or queried why we didn't have a BBQ (though, of course, some guests may have been disappointed but not told us). Several guests left the remains of a used disposable BBQ, so they brought their own.

On balance, I would say don't provide a BBQ unless your target market demands it. If you do decide to provide a BBQ, buy two. This allows you to have a clean BBQ at the Furnished Holiday Let while the other is at your home, being cleaned, ready to swap over when required.

If you garden is suitable, you could provide a fire pit. This doesn't need to be cleaned in the same way as a BBQ – your guests won't expect a spotless firepit. Some ashes and part burnt logs add to the story.

Think carefully about how many logs to supply – however many you supply, your guests will probably use them all. Perhaps leave a starter supply of logs, firelighters and kindling and, in your 'Guest Guide', indicate where your guests can buy further supplies.

NOTE: If you leave matches and firelighters to light a BBQ, Firepit, Wood Burner, Open Fire or anything else, make sure that you leave them out of the reach of children!

Another point to consider here is how much time you have to set up your Furnished Holiday Let. You must get the basics done first. Don't be led astray installing a hot tub or digging a firepit before you have fitted the kitchen and bought the furniture. Time can easily run away with you and you could find yourself with a wonderfully landscaped garden but no carpets in the property. By the time you've caught up with the basics, you could have missed the first month of the high season!

I know of one example where a cottage out in the countryside had a large, very overgrown garden/small field at the back. When the new owners started to clear the garden, they discovered a very large pond – a small lake really – fed by a natural spring. They decided to clear this out and market it to potential guests as an opportunity to go 'wild swimming' (or 'swimming' as we used to know it).

This was a fantastic USP (unique selling proposition) for their cottage and was certainly the right thing to do. But they had to be mindful not to spend so much time on the lake that the cottage refurbishment fell behind schedule. They were in a solid position financially, so didn't need to be concerned about the loss of income if they missed the first few weeks of the season - we aren't fortunate position!

You do need to give careful thought to the decoration of your Furnished Holiday Let. You might want to have some 'statement wallpaper walls' and have a unique theme to each bedroom. That's fine (and will help to gain your 5 stars, if that's what you're aiming for). But remember 'Practicality'. Your walls will inevitably be scratched by furniture, suitcases, shoes, etc. These will need to be touched up regularly. Marks on paintwork can easily be hidden with a few brush strokes. Tears in wallpaper provide more of a challenge. If you've painted every room in a different colour, your 'touching up' becomes more of a logistical exercise.

'Timeless' throughout, anyone?

Free Wifi is a 'must' these days. Your guests will expect to be able to log on to their devices and have a decent download speed. This is not something to cut corners on (should you cut corners on anything?). Your guests, adults and children, will probably search around for the Wifi code before they hang their clothes up in the wardrobes!

Think about rainy days. What will your guests do if they can't go to the beach or they don't fancy getting soaked walking across the moors? You need to provide some amusement for your guests to enjoy while they are indoors. At Rhubarb Cottage we provided a range of magazines, which we regularly updated (the magazines should be more recent than the ones that your guests will their doctor's surgery), a selection of books, of various genres to appeal to men, women and children, a Smart speaker, DVDs (and a DVD player, obvs), jigsaw puzzles and games.

A digital radio and/or Smart speaker (Alexa, play Virgin Radio) is expected now so that your guests can listen to a wide variety of radio stations and music.

What other 'extras' should you provide?

If your Furnished Holiday Let is by the sea, should you provide lilos, buckets and spades, crabbing nets and beach towels? If you are situated out in the countryside, should you provide binoculars and a bird spotting guide? Yes, of course you can, but you don't need to. If you do provide this sort of thing, though, it will be remembered by your guests. What you will almost certainly find is that as time progresses, your guests will leave various things for you, rather than take them home. We've found jigsaw puzzles that we hadn't bought, fishing lines, buckets and spades, magazines and books that didn't look familiar. If you provide fiction books, you may find that people will take them home if they haven't finished them. They will usually leave a different book to replace the one that they've taken. Alternatively, you might find that a parcel turns up at your house one day containing a book that's being returned to you!

If you are catering for families, you should provide a Highchair for babies and a Travel Cot with bedding. You can store these away when not required and set them up before the guests who need them arrive. You will need to ask if they require these at time of booking. A Stairgate is also useful.

If you're targeting dog owners, an outside tap is a 'must'. Add a length of hosepipe - one metre is enough - to enable the owners to wash down their dog before it goes into the house. Dog towels are also much appreciated. As is a dog bowl outside of the back door, filled with water.

Dogs tend to get muddy (sometimes very muddy) so it's important that the guests can clean them down before they come into the property. When they do come in, they'll probably still be wet, so having an area where they can be kept until they are dry is very useful. The kitchen will do for this but if you have a separate area with a hard floor, that would be better. At Rhubarb Cottage we had an entrance hall with a parquet wood block floor. Guests left their dogs in this area to dry out before coming into the rest of the cottage.

Walkers also appreciate an outside tap to clean their walking boots. At Rhubarb Cottage, the walkers also left their (cleaned, but wet) boots in the hallway. A boot scraper is also useful to get the worst of the mud off the soles of boots.

Cyclists need somewhere safe to store their bikes. A shed is fine. Most cyclists will have their own cycle locks, although we did provide one, in case of need. Cyclists, too, will look for an outside tap to clean their bikes and shoes.

If you have a garden with plants that need to be watered, attach a complete hosepipe to the outside tap. Politely ask your guests if they could water the plant pots and flower beds a couple of times during the week. Some will enjoy doing that, others won't bother, but at least you will be helping to keep the plants going.

If you have a washing machine but no tumble drier, you need to provide a washing line and pegs. Retractable washing lines are best as these are virtually hidden when not in use. Many of your guests will use the washing line, if only to dry their tea towels and the dog towels.

Inside the cottage, try to set up a small area where you can display leaflets from local attractions and places of interest. You can pick up these leaflets at a local tourism shop or direct from the attractions. This will be well received by your guests.

Buy a Visitors' Book. Your happy guests will write a few lines thanking you for your hospitality and telling you what a wonderful time they've had (sometimes adding 'in spite of the weather'). Other guests like to read the Visitors' Book and it's a very positive promotional tool for your Furnished Holiday Let.

If a guest has had an issue when they stayed in your property, or something wasn't up to their expectation, they will contact you or leave you a note of explanation. You will obviously deal with this, as appropriate. At Rhubarb Cottage, in the 15 years that we ran the cottage we only had one guest who wrote about an issue in the Visitors' Book. This was disappointing for us as future guests could read it, even though it was actually a misunderstanding and easily rectified.

You can be pretty sure that your Visitors' Book will be full of positive messages!

Some Furnished Holiday Lets advertise that they provide a Welcome Pack for their guests. This will contain items such as bread, butter, milk, tea, coffee, sugar, eggs, a bottle of wine, dog biscuits, a cake, etc. A range of staples to enable the guests to make a cup of tea and have a slice of toast when they arrived. If you decide to do this, try to source produce locally. That is always appreciated by your guests and it cuts down on the 'food miles' used to supply the produce.

At Rhubarb Cottage we supplied a Welcome Pack containing the items listed above. The difference was that we never advertised the fact that we would be supplying the Welcome Pack. It was a nice surprise for our guests to find the unexpected Welcome Pack and we had lots of positive comments about it in our Visitors' Book.

HOWEVER, you may, or may not, be surprised to know that there are laws that apply to the provision of food and drink hampers in relation to both food hygiene, labelling, allergens etc.

You almost certainly will be surprised to know that, by law, if you buy or make an alcoholic drink (sloe gin, home brew beer, etc) which you then leave for your guests as part of a Welcome Hamper, you need to be licensed!

So why is leaving a bottle of wine for a guest different from taking a bottle to a friend's party? The difference is that your Furnished Holiday Let is a business. Your guests have paid for their accommodation. The provision of the alcohol can be seen as an "incentive to purchase" so someone might book your accommodation rather than a similar cottage up the road because you provide this. Also, the guests only get the alcohol when they stay which means, in effect, they have paid for the alcohol within the price of their holiday.

I've never heard of anyone being prosecuted for providing a bottle of wine in a Welcome Hamper, but there is always a chance that it could happen.

You also need to ensure that everything in your Welcome Hamper contains details of any allergens in case any of your guests have an allergy. This also (particularly) applies to any home made produce that you provide.

If you would like to read more about this, check here:

https://www.pascuk.co.uk/wp-content/uploads/2021/09/Welcome-Hampers-PASC-UK-Sept-21.pdf

Appendix 5 gives you a suggested checklist of things that you need/ought to include in your Furnished Holiday Let.

Setting up your Administration

This is an important topic which you need to consider carefully during your set up stage. If you have decided to manage your Furnished Holiday Let through an agent, then much of this section will not apply to you. If you are going to run the business yourself and keep the 20%+ commission that the agent would have charged you, then read on!

What documentation will you need to set up to keep track of the business?

Booking Schedule

What will you do when you receive a booking? You will need a Booking Schedule to which you will add the name of the guest against the dates that they have booked – usually a week.

NOTE: This is not the same as a Booking Calendar, which you will have on your website (see later).

The Booking Schedule contains information that you need to manage all of your bookings together, so that you don't double book a particular week.

The Booking Calendar is for potential guests to see when you have vacancies and how much each week/weekend costs, throughout the year.

At Rhubarb Cottage we had a template for the Booking Schedule with headings as follows:

Date, Name, Length of Stay, Number in the party, Changeover Day, Contact Phone Number, Dog? Travel Cot? Highchair? Been Before? Price, Notes

Most of that is self-explanatory. Changeover Day will usually be Friday or Saturday. However, in the Low season you will have some weeks where you rent out a part week – Monday to Thursday perhaps. Your changeover days will be Monday and Thursday. If you employ a cleaner, it's important that they know that they will be needed on those days and given plenty of notice. We updated our Booking Schedule each time we received a booking and we regularly photocopied it and gave the copy to the lady that often helped us with the cleaning, so that she knew when she might be called upon to help.

It's important to make a note of whether your guests have been before. If they have, you can refer to their previous visit when you correspond with them.

In the Notes section, you can record anything of interest that happened during the stay – good or bad. If that guest books again, you know what to expect. 'Left the cottage spotless' is always a nice note to record after the guests have left. 'The place was a tip' is not so great and you might think twice before accepting a return visit from that guest.

An example of this template can be seen in Appendix 6

Invoice Template

Your guest has booked. You now need to send them an invoice for the deposit. The invoice is also confirmation that you have accepted the booking. Your customers will need to know how much to pay you, when and how.

At Rhubarb Cottage, we asked for 25% of the total payment at the time of booking, with the balance due 6 weeks before the holiday guests were due to arrive.

Any bookings within the 6 weeks were required to pay the full amount at the time of booking.

You will need to set up an invoice template and a numbering system, to keep track of payments due to you.

Receipt of Payment

We accepted payments by cheque or by bank transfer. You will need to include your bank details on your invoice.

We did not accept credit card payments, as these were expensive to set up for one holiday property. You may feel that you would like to accept credit cards, to make payments easy for your customers. Payment terminals are more readily available now at a reasonable price – Google 'How can I accept credit cards for my small business?' (or something similar) and you will see a number of options that are available.

When you receive a payment, you need to confirm receipt back to your guest. We did this by updating the invoice to confirm receipt.

Directions to your property and how to gain access

Before your guests arrive, you will send them directions on how to find the property and obtain the key. This may include a map and postcode, for the satnav.

You can also include a what3words reference. what3words has divided the world into 3 metre squares and given each square a unique combination of three random words.
what3words addresses are easy to say and share, and as accurate as GPS coordinates. The maps are accessed through an App on your mobile phone. Search Google Play or the Apple Store for what3words.

When your guests arrive, how will they collect the front door key? You might meet the guests when they arrive to welcome them and hand over the key, or you might have another method to enable them to collect the key. You could leave the key with a neighbour (not recommended, unless in an emergency). At Rhubarb Cottage, we used a key safe, which had a combination lock. We changed the combination numbers every week and confirmed the new number to the guests before they arrived. In this way, our guests could arrive at any time, to suit them.

HOW TO SET UP AND RUN A SELF-CATERING
HOLIDAY PROPERTY

A Guests' Guide to your property

When your guests have arrived, they need to know where to find everything and orientate themselves. It is good practice to put together a manual which would contain information such as:

Safety Instructions

Where to find things in the property

Useful telephone numbers

Things to do in the area

Interesting information on the history of the property (if relevant)

Nearest supermarkets, with directions

Recommendations for restaurants and pubs (with a caveat that things may have changed since you last visited, in case your guests are disappointed)

Dog friendly pubs and places of interest

Etc

A suggested Guests' Guide can be seen in Appendix 7

You can leave the Guest' Guide in a prominent position in your Furnished Holiday Let, so that your new guests can see it when they arrive. The dining room table is an obvious place, but you may have a better position for it.

HOWEVER, as I have mentioned earlier, don't assume that all of your guests will read your words of wisdom. Most will flick through the document and 'file it away' on the top of the sideboard, never to be revisited.

This leaves you with the issue of how to ensure that your guests know how to use the facilities. If you have an Aga in the kitchen, for example, you will know that one of the hotplates is the 'boiling' hotplate and one is the 'simmering' hotplate. Similarly, you will know which oven is the 'baking' oven and which is the 'warming' oven. Will your guests know this? If they have an aga at home, then they will. Most of your guests will never have used an aga, so they certainly won't know how to use it.

Will your guests know how to operate your new Nespresso machine (the one that you have purchased to help towards qualifying for your 4 star quality rating)? Will they know that they may have to press the top lever down quite hard to force the coffee capsule down into the machine? Again, if they have a similar machine at home, they will know. If they don't, they won't want to apply too much force to push the coffee capsule into position in case they break the machine and so they won't use it. They might phone you up to ask about using the machine. Worse, they might leave an unnecessarily bad review on TripAdvisor.

To overcome this, I would recommend that you prepare a sheet of instructions for each item in the property that requires some explanation. Ideally, laminate these instruction sheets.

The individual laminated instructions should then be left in the property in the appropriate position close to each item, to remind guests what they need to do. These might include:

> Managing and recycling waste (example see Appendix 1)
>
> How to light the log burner (example see Appendix 8)
>
> How to use the DAB radio and Smart Speaker
>
> How to access the Wifi (example see Appendix 9)
>
> Etc

Feedback Questionnaire

How do you know how well you are doing? Are you providing what your guests are expecting, or could you do better? One way to find out is to leave a blank feedback questionnaire at your Furnished Holiday Let so that your guests can give you that feedback – good and bad.

This doesn't need to be a complicated form. It could be as simple as:

> HOW TO SET UP AND RUN A SELF-CATERING
> HOLIDAY PROPERTY

> Please rate your overall experience 1 – 10, where 1 is awful and 10 is excellent.

> In the space provided, please leave any comments to help us to give our guests a great holiday experience.

You can ask for a name and date of stay. Make this optional, as some people will prefer to take the form home and send it to you anonymously, particularly if they have some negative points to highlight.

Another option is to ask:

> Please rate your overall experience 1 – 10, where 1 is awful and 10 is excellent.

> What should we continue to do?

> What should we do more of?

> What should we do less of?

The majority of your guests won't bother to complete the form. Those that do, though, will give you valuable feedback which will help you to improve the holiday experience for your future guests.

Vacating the property

Your guests need to know the time by which they must leave and any special instructions about what to do with the key, for example. You should confirm this in correspondence at the time of booking but it's advisable to leave a note in the property, in an obvious place such as on the table, so that your guests are reminded when to leave.

A Dummy Run

When you have fitted out your Furnished Holiday Let and set up your admin, you are ready to start advertising your property and receive your first guests. Before you take in your first guest you would be well advised to have a 'dummy run' or 'snagging trip' to identify any issues before your guests find them.

You can do this yourself or better, ask a friend to do this for you.

You should run through exactly what your guests will do. Park where your guests will park, find the key, enter the property with a suitcase. Walk around as a guest would do. Flick through the Guests' Guide. Make a cup of coffee. Watch TV, send an email, which will require logging in to the Wifi. Luxuriate in the bath. Cook an evening meal. Stay the night at the property and sleep in the main bedroom. Have a shower in the morning, etc etc.

You might be surprised what you find. Did you know how to light the log burner? Did you find the instructions next to the log burner or were they only in the Guests' Guide?

> HOW TO SET UP AND RUN A SELF-CATERING HOLIDAY PROPERTY

Was the Wifi easy to set up? If not, was there a cable that your guests could use as a backup?

While you were lying in the bath did you see any cobwebs on the ceiling or any 'unfinished' tile grouting which isn't visible unless you are lying down?

When it's dark outside, is the lighting in the property bright enough? Is it sufficient to allow your guests to relax on the sofa and read a book, or do you need a reading lamp?

Have you left a kitchen cupboard empty to allow people somewhere to store their food?

Are there any spare blankets in case your guests are cold at night?

Etc, etc.

A Dummy Run is definitely time well spent.

Setting up your Commercials

Setting up your price schedule

How do you know how much to charge for a week/weekend at your Furnished Holiday Let? The market will determine how much you can charge at different times of the year. The best way to get a feel for this is to look at your competitors' pricing. Assess how your property stacks up against each competitor and price your property accordingly.

Do not make the mistake of thinking that you should undercut your competitors. You are not selling packaged groceries or TVs – the more of these that are sold, the higher the turnover. You have one week to sell at any one time in the year. Once that week has been booked, you can't sell it again. So, you need to maximise your pricing to maximise your profits. Remember, it's not a race to get your property booked up first before your competitors. The prize is to make the most profit.

In any specific week, your competitors' properties might all be booked up before yours gets a booking. But you might have set a higher price and made more profit.

Sometimes, of course, some of your weeks aren't booked as quickly as you would hope. As you get nearer to the date you can reduce the price, to make the package more attractive. If you do this, show the price change as a 'Late Availability price reduction', rather than knocking £50 off of the price in your booking calendar (see the Marketing section later).

For example – your published price for w/c 12th August (peak season) is £1,195. In the middle of July, the week is still not booked and you decide to reduce the price by £100. On your website, insert a announcement 'w/c 12th August - Late Availability - £100 discount!'

This will have a greater impact than adjusting your price to £1,095 on the booking calendar.

Your price should include all utilities, including Wifi – don't charge extra for this. It should also include all bedding and towels unless you ask your guests to bring their own. You can ask for an extra payment if your guests wish to bring a pet. This is usually a dog, or dogs. At Rhubarb Cottage over the years, in addition to dogs of all sizes we had cats, a parrot, budgies, house rabbits, guinea pigs and a tortoise!

We charged £25 per pet per week. Almost everyone is fine with paying this. When we had returning guests who had been before, we often gave their pets a free holiday, which was always appreciated. If a potential guest is hesitating to make a booking, you can offer not to charge for their pet, which might make the difference between them making a booking or your enquiring guest looking elsewhere.

Refundable Damage Deposit

You should ask your guests to pay a refundable damage deposit, payable when the balance of the monies is due. At Rhubarb Cottage, we asked for £75 but this could easily be increased to £100. If there is no damage caused by your guests while they are staying in your Holiday Let you will refund their damage deposit in full. If some serious damage has occurred, you can agree some compensation with your guest and deduct the agreed amount from your refund.

I would not advise charging your guests for things like a broken glass or a scuff on the wall – these are part and parcel of running a Furnished Holiday Let, I'm afraid.

Tracking your expenditure

Your Furnished Holiday Let is a business, not a hobby. If you have made a profit at the end of the year, HMRC will expect an income tax payment from you. So, you need to keep detailed records of your expenditure and your income.

You will be able to find an off the shelf finance package which you can use to keep a track of your expenses and income. Alternatively, you can set up a spreadsheet with a tab for each month. Within each tab, set up a section for Outgoings and leave about 20 blank rows. Below this, set up a similar section for Income – you won't need as many blank rows for this, sadly.

Along the top of the Outgoings section, add in appropriate headings to identify the type of expenditure. These will be something like - Total (the sum of all the columns), Decoration and Repairs, Insurance, Travelling Expenses, Mortgage, Business Rates, Fees, Furniture & Fittings, Advertising, Utilities, Damage Deposit Refunds, Weekly Maintenance, Miscellaneous.

Along the top of the Incomings section, add in appropriate headings to identify the type of expenditure – Total, Rent, Refundable Damage Deposit Other.

The spreadsheet will look something like this:

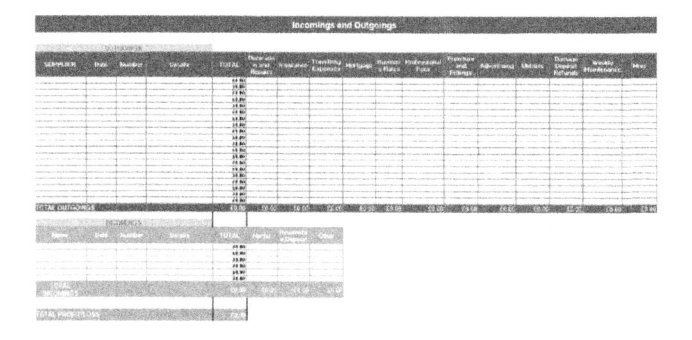

Several of the entries will be Direct Debits and can be filled in for every month at the start of the year.

Most expenditure will be ad hoc. Try and get into the routine of updating the spreadsheet as you go along, rather than bunging all of your receipts in a box and then trying to sort them out at the end of the year. It is much easier that way!

Terms and Conditions

You will need to draw up a set of Terms and Conditions (T&Cs) that your potential guests can see before they book (if they bother to read them, of course). As well as informing your potential guests of 'the rules in your Furnished Holiday Let', your T&Cs cover you in the event of your guests doing something that they shouldn't. If an official body such as the police becomes involved in an issue, your T&Cs will show that you are on the side of right.

Your T&Cs will include what you expect from your guests. If you don't accept single sex groups, say so in your T&Cs. If you do not allow your guests to have a party while they are staying in your Furnished Holiday Let, include this in the T&Cs.

If the worst happens and your guests break one of your rules, you can point to your T&Cs and expect some recompense.

You can see a copy of our T&Cs at Rhubarb Cottage in Appendix 10. You could, of course, adapt these for your own use.

Changeover Day

Before you begin advertising your property you will need to decide on your Changeover Day. This will either be a Friday or a Saturday. It doesn't really matter which one you choose from a potential guests' point of view. You will get bookings whichever you choose, so it's really a matter of personal choice for you.

A Saturday changeover is most common. If you are working full time Monday – Friday and you are doing the changeover yourself, then you will have no choice but to choose a Saturday. The disadvantage of a Saturday changeover is that it ties you down over the weekend. If you want to go away for a short weekend break, you can't leave until later on Saturday, unless you can find someone else to cover the changeover for you.

A Friday changeover is becoming increasingly common. The benefit of a Friday changeover is that it lends itself to 'Long Weekend' bookings – Friday pm – Sunday or Monday am. You want to avoid weekend bookings in the high season but you will need to take weekend and midweek bookings outside of the high season – you won't have as many full week bookings during these months.

Once you have decided on your changeover day, you need to decide on timings – what time can guests arrive and depart. Remember that you have to complete the property turnaround in the hours between guests.

Asking guests to depart by 10am is common, no later. You could ask guests to leave by 9am, but that might put some people off from booking your property.

Allowing guests to arrive from 2pm was common until Covid-19 appeared. Now, with the increased time required to clean and sanitise the property, it is usual to allow guests to arrive from 3pm. Some Furnished Holiday Lets state from 4pm. Guests understand that cleanliness and sanitising are vitally important, so very few will quibble if they can't gain access until 4pm (if they do quibble, they're likely to complain about other things too ...).

Building your Support Network

Once your Furnished Holiday Let is up and running you will be relying on other people to help you. As well as someone to help with the cleaning, perhaps, you will also need the services of skilled tradesmen. You should try and find good local tradesmen for all eventualities, so that you can call on them in time of need. This list will include:

- Electrician
- Gas Engineer
- Plumber
- Small Builder
- Window Cleaner
- Oven Cleaning Company
- Carpenter and Fitter
- Tiler
- Gardener
- Vehicle Mechanic
- Carpet Fitter
- Handyman for odd jobs

You should also think about suppliers to your business. You may be able to negotiate a discount with some of these, particularly if you are (or will be) a regular customer.

What will happen at your Furnished Holiday Let if you are ill? Do you have a backup plan? You need to have a fall-back person(s) who you can call upon to help out with changeovers if you are not able to do it yourself. This could be your partner, other family member or friend. Try and line up a couple of people who can help you out when you're desperate!

Your support network could also include Insurance. Depending on your attitude to Risk, you might want to take out Boiler Breakdown Insurance which gives you 24/7 cover. This will give you peace of mind that if your boiler breaks down, it will be quickly fixed (in theory, at any rate. Sometimes, 'parts' take a long time to arrive). You might also consider insurance against your kitchen appliances breaking down – your oven, washing machine, fridge, etc.

These insurance policies are, of course, over and above the Landlord's Insurance which you must have and which will cover you for any legal liabilities.

Marketing your Furnished Holiday Let

'Build a better mousetrap, and the world will beat a path to your door' is a quotation attributed to Ralph Waldo Emerson in the late 1800s. In fact, it is a misquote but the sentiment remains – if you have something that's better than its competitors, people will want to find you and buy it.

That may have been true in the 19th century but sadly, is not true today. You can have the best Furnished Holiday Let in your area but if nobody knows about it, nobody will come and stay in it. You need to be proactive and tell people all about your lovely accommodation and how it's just what they're looking for.

You have decided on your target market, so you know who you would like to see your marketing messages. But how do you reach them?

Developing a website

The first thing that you should consider is to set up a website. This can seem rather daunting if you have never done this before but there are plenty of people that can help you. You have the choice of developing the website yourself or paying others to do it for you. There are plenty of agencies and freelancers who will be more than happy to develop a website for you. There will be local agencies in your area, almost certainly. This the best way to proceed if you don't have the time or the expertise to develop a website yourself but, of course, this will be the most expensive route.

If you do decide to employ an agency, my strong advice is to get your brief finalised before any work starts. They will come back to you with a mock up of the website – they will call it a 'wireframe'. You will then need to agree the copy and images to be used. Make any changes as early in the process as you can. The later you make changes, the more expensive they become (because the changes will involve more work).

Make sure that your website is 'Responsive'. This means that it will fit properly to the size of the screen, whether it is viewed on a PC, a laptop, a tablet or a mobile phone.

You don't need a complicated website – you aren't competing with Amazon! As a rough guide, you need:

>Home Page

>About the property

>Gallery

>Make a Booking (a form)

>Contact Us (a form)

>Testimonials (to follow as you get some!)

>Interesting points about the area

> HOW TO SET UP AND RUN A SELF-CATERING
> HOLIDAY PROPERTY

Terms and Conditions

Blog (see later)

This will be a very easy website for your agency to produce. So easy, in fact that you could develop it yourself!

There are several software packages and websites that can provide you with website templates, which are your starting point.

Amateur web developers who have some experience tend to prefer a package such as Wordpress. This is relatively easy to get to grips with and if you were developing a complex site, I would recommend this route.

There are other, simpler, packages that will suit your purposes to develop a website which will tell the world about your Furnished Holiday Let. At Rhubarb Cottage, we used Wix.

www.wix.com

The Wix website has hundreds of templates from which you can choose one that you like. You can change almost every element on the templates, take elements out and add others in. It's mostly 'drag and drop' and quite easy to learn. There is a wide range of Apps that you can also add, but you won't need to worry too much about those for your website.

The basic Wix package is free but the free version will show adverts on your website. If you want to take off the adverts and also have access to a wide range of other Apps and functions, there is an annual fee. This is not expensive and a worthwhile investment, to make your website look more professional.

If you take this route, I suggest that you review the websites of properties that are similar to your own. Pick up ideas and incorporate these into your own website.

The two most important things to get right on your website are your images and your booking calendar.

Your images must be the best that you can manage. You might even decide to get a professional photographer in to do this for you – money well spent. Your images are your big selling point, they are often the guest's first impression of a property. The majority of your potential guests will scroll through your images before they read your copy – if they don't like what they see, they won't get as far as reading your pearls of wisdom.

As well as images of your property, inside and out, try to include some of the local area, particularly if your Furnished Holiday Let is in a scenic part of the country.

Potential guests need to see your availability and how much it costs to rent a particular week/weekend. Make this easy for them. Don't say something like 'For current availability and prices, please contact us on xxxxxxxx'. People won't bother to do that, they'll look elsewhere.

Keep your booking calendar up to date. Another common 'faux pas' is not keeping your calendar updated and a potential guest makes an online booking for a week that's actually already booked. You have to go back to the potential guest and apologise for the mix up. Not great.

Why should a potential guest choose to stay in your area? When you write the copy for your website, don't forget to include a section or a page on local attractions and sights. You might have a theme park near you, which will be very popular with families. You could be near a large country house which is open to the public. This will be popular with older visitors.

Also, when developing your copy, think about what your guests will do on rainy days. Include indoor attractions nearby that can be visited if the weather lets you down.

You will almost certainly have some excellent restaurants in your area. Put a link to their websites on your website – this will all help to bring traffic to your website and potential guests will be grateful for the local insights.

Hosting the website

You will need to find a host for your website, for which you will pay an annual fee. If you employ an agency to develop your website, they will be able to arrange the hosting for you.

If you go down the Wix route, hosting is included in their package, which makes life easier for you.

Hosting companies include:

www.ionos.co.uk

www.uk2.net

www.bluehost.com

www.hostinger.co.uk

and many others

Choosing a Domain Name

The domain name is the name of the website and the wording that you click on to open a website. In the example of the Hosts above, www.ionos.co.uk is the domain name.

Your choice of domain name is very important. A potential guest might search for 'Holiday cottages in the lake district takes dogs'. When Google and other search engines search the web for suitable websites that relate to the search query, they rank websites based on complex algorithms. One of the considerations is whether any of the words in the search query are included in the website's domain name.

If your domain name is

www.holidaycottagesinthelakedistricttakesdogs.co.uk

your website will almost certainly rank quite highly in your potential guest's search results. (The link above does not go to a website because …… at the time of writing, that domain name is available to buy! If you have a Furnished Holiday Let in the Lake District that is dog friendly, why not snap it up?)

Most of the simple domain names that you would like to use will already have been taken by somebody else. You should think about the typical search queries that potential guests will use to find a Furnished Holiday Let like yours, in your area. Test some of those, to see if the domain is available.

You can have more than one domain name. Some organisations have many domain names which all point to the same website. In the example above, a Holiday Let in the Lake District might already have the domain www.lakedistrictholidays.co.uk They could register another domain name and point both domains at the same website. In that way, they are more likely to rank higher in searches.

The Hosting companies listed above, and many others, will register a domain name for you. The fee is not expensive and you will need to renew it every 1 or 2 years.

At the time of writing www.UK2.net has a domain name checker on the home page. You can enter a proposed domain name into the checker and see if it is still available. You will often find that the .com version has been taken but the .co.uk and other variants are still available.

Don't worry about your domain name being too long. Yes, shorter is better and easier to remember but 9 times out of 10, your potential guests will click on a link rather than typing out your domain name. At Rhubarb Cottage we had two domains:

www.escapetothenewforest.co.uk

and

www.holidaycottagesinnewforest.co.uk   (now no longer in use)

Your website has to be 'pointed' to your hosted domain. Your agency will do this for you. If you take the DIY route such as Wix, the instructions to tell you how to do this are quite straightforward.

Using Directories

Google and other search engines always prioritise directories over individual websites. This is one of the reasons that it is so difficult for individual businesses to appear on the first search page. The first entries in most searches are 'paid for advertisements', which makes the first page even harder to reach. 'Paid for' advertisements have an **Ad** symbol in the title line, usually the first three and the last three on the page.

As a result of this, you really need to add your Furnished Holiday Let to a selection of Directories, which will then link back to your website. Some of these are free, most charge you an annual fee.

TripAdvisor

The best known of these directories is TripAdvisor. In the UK, the website www.holidaylettings.co.uk is used to feature self-catering accommodation. You add your Furnished Holiday Let to this site and your property will also appear on TripAdvisor.

TripAdvisor has two models, one is free, the other has an annual fee. The main difference comes in the pricing of your accommodation. Potential guests can book direct through TripAdvisor – you may have done this yourself in the past when you've booked a holiday. If you use the free version of TripAdvisor, a number of fees will be added to the total price shown in the directory. These additional fees will be deducted by TripAdvisor before they pay you, the holiday home owner.

If you use the 'fee' version of TripAdvisor, these booking fees are not added. I would recommend going with the free version to start with. If you find you receive a significant number of bookings through TripAdvisor, you might want to move to the 'fee' version.

Airbnb

Airbnb is an example of the 'sharing economy', like Uber, where underutilised resources are shared. Uber is a software platform where drivers can register to use their own vehicle as a taxi. Airbnb is a software platform on which homeowners can advertise their spare room(s) for rent. Both of these companies and others, seek to enable people to maximise the use of their own resources, hence the 'sharing economy'.

Airbnb was originally set up, as above, to enable people with a spare room to rent out their room to guests to raise some extra cash. Many of the entries on Airbnb are still exactly that. However, once Airbnb became established as a mainstream holiday directory, a significant number of Furnished Holiday Lets (and hotels and B&Bs) started to advertise on the platform. This now extends the reach of Airbnb outside of the 'sharing economy' and into the mainstream holiday market.

Airbnb is different from other directories, though, as it is still used by those people for whom it was originally set up – people with a spare room to rent, people who are effectively 'amateurs'.

Since covid-19 came along, cleaning and hygiene standards have been massively ramped up. Do all of the owners offering single night stays follow the covid-19 standards? Do people who advertise their spare room have the appropriate insurance?

You need to be comfortable that this is the right directory for you to use to advertise your Furnished Holiday Let.

Both TripAdvisor and Airbnb have been applauded for refunding holidaymakers in full if they can't take their holiday for some reason, including Covid-19 related lockdowns. Airbnb will refund the booker right up until the day before the guests were due to arrive.

It's a very generous policy on their part. Not really. It's not their money that they're refunding, it's yours! If Airbnb refunds a cancellation the day before the guest was due to arrive you have no chance of reletting the property. Neither do you have the option of offering the guest the option of moving their booking to a later date, which some guests would like to do.

No, you lose the money ...

But you can avoid this. Both TripAdvisor and Airbnb have a scale of cancellation policies from 'Relaxed' or 'Flexible' to 'Super Strict'.

On TripAdvisor, the 'Relaxed' policy allows for 100% refunds if a cancellation is made at least two weeks before the start date of the holiday.

On Airbnb, the 'Flexible' policy allows for 100% refunds if a cancellation is made up to the day before the start date of the holiday.

On both directories, you can select a stricter cancellation policy which will allow you to retain an increasing percentage of the cost of the holiday when a guest cancels at a late stage. If you set up your Furnished Holiday Let on these directories, make sure that you choose the policy that you feel happy with, don't accept the default.

There are numerous other directories. One that we have found very productive in the past is Love to Escape:

www.lovetoescape.com

Another is My Favourite Holiday Cottages:

www.myfavouriteholidaycottages.co.uk

You will also find very good directories that focus on your local area. For Rhubarb Cottage, we joined the local tourism group:

www.thenewforest.co.uk

It's a good idea to subscribe to a local directory. Your main competitors will probably be there, and you will also keep up with all developments relating to tourism in the local area.

A Google search will turn up plenty more directories. The majority of these will be companies that do everything for you, that we reviewed earlier. These are the companies that manage your bookings and your weekly changeovers but charge you 20% and more for their services. If you have chosen to take this route with your Furnished Holiday Let, then your property will already be on their directory.

One other point to mention here is that, if you have a website and you join, say, three directories, you will have four different booking calendars to maintain. Most of the directories will offer you the option of using their booking calendar on your website and, in some cases, on other directories.

This is a great time saver and worth considering – you only have to update one calendar. The only downside is that you will pay the booking calendar website's booking fees, even for bookings that are made through your own website.

Social Media

No marketing plan would be complete without encompassing social media. We hear a lot about it, but what is social media?

Oxford Languages defines social media as 'websites and applications that enable users to create and share content or to participate in social networking'.

Here are some suggestions on how you could utilise social media to promote your Holiday Let:

Facebook

The first application that will come to mind for most people is Facebook. 42 million people in the UK have a Facebook account. That's out of a total population (adults and children) of about 67 million. It's quite popular then!

Almost none of the Facebook users will be below the age of 30 – they use Instagram, Snapchat, TikTok and others. This shouldn't concern you, though, as the target market for your Furnished Holiday Let is almost certainly in the mid to older age groups.

You are probably one of the 42 million. You have your own Facebook Newsfeed, where you see posts by friends, family and the groups to which you belong. Did you know, though, that you can also have Business Facebook Pages? These are separate from your own Facebook Page. You can set up a page for your business – your Furnished Holiday Let.

This is a free way of promoting your holiday property to a wide audience. Anyone who 'likes' one of the posts on your business page (not your personal page) will see your future business page posts appear in their Newsfeed. You can also 'Boost' your individual business page posts. You can choose the audience who you want to receive your business page posts based on a number of parameters provided by Facebook.

In the example below, I have imagined that my Furnished Holiday Let is a holiday cottage in Devon. I have chosen an audience of:

> HOW TO SET UP AND RUN A SELF-CATERING HOLIDAY PROPERTY

Men and women aged 30 – 65+ (this is not visible in the image below)

People living in the UK within the ages above

People who like dog walking and the countryside

People who have an interest in Devon and going to the beach

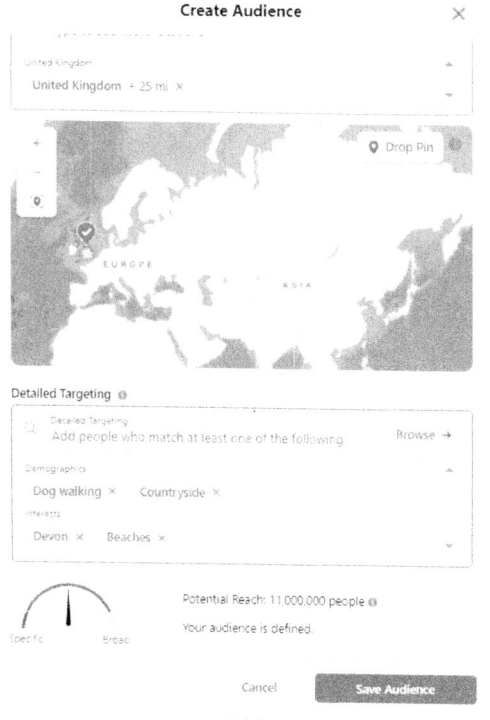

This gives us a potential reach of 11 million people who could be interested in booking the holiday cottage in Devon.

You then set your budget and press 'Boost'. Once approved by Facebook, your boosted post will appear in the Newsfeeds of Facebook users who fall within the audience that you have defined. This is a great way of promoting your Furnished Holiday Let at minimal cost. I recommend that you do this.

This also explains why you see various posts in your own Facebook Newsfeed from individuals and organisations that you have never heard of – you have been targeted by these organisations, who think that you might be interested in whatever it is that they are offering.

Instagram

If you take photos on your mobile phone, Instagram is another good way to promote your Furnished Holiday Let. Instagram is set up for users to share their photos. Most people look at the images and rarely read any supporting text beyond the image title.

You cannot add a link to your website in Instagram posts. However, you can add a website link in your Instagram Bio (your biography in your My Account section). So, you can direct people to the link in your Bio when you post your pictures.

Instagram is owned by Facebook, so you can set up your Instagram feed to automatically share your posts on

Facebook as well. So, posting on Instagram allows you to post the same message on Facebook.

If you don't take photos on your phone, I wouldn't bother with Instagram.

Twitter

Twitter is probably the most controversial of the major social media apps. It is the app that allows instant feedback about anything and plenty of celebrities and people in the public eye have found themselves at the centre of a 'Twitterstorm' when they have said or done something that a lot of people don't agree with.

Twitter is an 'echo chamber' where people will generally see tweets that they agree with (because the Twitter algorithms show you tweets that they think you will be interested in, which tend to be tweets that you agree with). This leads to Twitter users thinking that nearly everybody agrees with them, and they are then surprised to find that, out in the real world, this is generally not the case.

You can use Twitter to promote your Furnished Holiday Let by regularly 'tweeting' about anything relevant to your target audience. You will gradually build up a following, particularly if you engage with other Twitter users.

You can also set up your Instagram feed to automatically share your posts on Twitter. If you use Instagram, I recommend that you do this.

Twitter can be very time consuming (and addictive). Personally, I wouldn't recommend using Twitter to promote your Furnished Holiday Let unless you are already a Twitter user.

Blogging

If you have the time, writing a blog is another good way to promote your Furnished Holiday Let and keep a dialogue going with potential guests. You can write about your property – things you've updated, things you've changed, etc. You can also write about your local area and what's going on.

Promoting forthcoming local events is also another topic that you can include in your blog. Of course, you can also tell your readers about any Late Availability offers that you have, which will also encourage readers to subscribe to your blog.

If you do decide to write a blog, you need, ideally, to keep up a regular output of new material. Once a fortnight is fine, once a month is OK. Each piece doesn't need to be too long but I would urge you to include images in each blog. People love to look at pictures and your blog will have much greater appeal if you include images.

The best place to host your blog is on your website, if you have one. This would form another section on the website. Search engines look for updated material on websites all the time and if you are adding new blog posts regularly, your website will achieve a higher position in the search rankings.

Google

As well as using Google as a search engine, you can also register your Furnished Holiday Let on Google. In Google's own words:

Start the process of adding your business to Google Maps by signing up for or logging into Google My Business, then follow the simple instructions to claim or create your free Business Profile on Google. Your Business Profile on Google is a free business listing from Google My Business, that allows you to show up in local search and on Google Maps.

You'll be asked to fill in some basic information about your business, such as:

- *location/address*
- *category*
- *website*
- *phone number*
- *opening hours*

You can also choose and claim a short name and URL for your listing. The information that appears in your Business Profile on Google will be shown on Google Maps and in results from Google Search, either when users make a search using relevant keywords or are looking for specific information about your business.

A business listing for your business may already exist on Google Maps if past customers have left you a review or uploaded a photo. If this is the case, you'll need to claim the listing (rather than creating it from scratch) and verify that you own the business before you can make changes to the information displayed in your profile.

When you have your Business Profile set up on Google, it is very important for you to complete all of the sections. Research shows that almost 70% of users view businesses with complete listings as more reputable, approachable and well-established. The more complete your business listing is, the more effective it will be – giving you a better chance of attracting new guests to your Furnished Holiday Let.

Like TripAdvisor and others, your guests can leave you a review on Google. More reviews will mean a higher ranking in search results so try and increase the number of positive reviews from your happy guests.

Once you are established you will receive regular updates from Google (unless you opt out). This is useful information, as it tells you the top search queries that people used when looking for a suitable holiday property. Here is an example from Rhubarb Cottage:

> HOW TO SET UP AND RUN A SELF-CATERING
> HOLIDAY PROPERTY

Google My Business

Rhubarb Cottage

6,816 PEOPLE FOUND YOU ON GOOGLE

Here are the top search queries used to find you:

self catering new forest	new forest self catering dog friendly	dog friendly cottages
used by 81 people	used by 67 people	used by 47 people

You can use this information to 'tweak' the copy on your website, making sure that these key search terms are included (maybe more than once) in the description of your property.

Other Promotional Opportunities

Your guests

There is no better ambassador for your property (or any product or service) than a happy customer. If you delight your guests, they are likely to come back and stay in your property again. They are also likely to tell their friends and family, who might also fancy a holiday in your area and who would be likely to book with you.

To encourage guests to return, you could give them a money off voucher when they leave, which they could redeem against another visit to your property within the next e.g. 12 months. Make sure you put an end date on the voucher, otherwise you might find somebody turning up several years later, expecting to redeem their voucher. You should also number the vouchers to discourage photocopying.

You could also make the voucher redeemable only in the low season, to try to increase bookings at that time of year. If you do that, you need to make the offer quite generous – but why not? Better to have a booking in December at a lower rate than no booking at all. You get the booking, your returning guests get a bargain, everyone's happy!

Testimonials

When you purchase things online, do you look at the testimonials that have been added by previous purchasers? Most people do. We know that some of these might be fake. We also know that some suppliers will 'incentivise' people who have entered negative comments to delete their comments or to update them, after their query has been satisfied.

What we can be sure of, is that if a product has a high number of very positive comments, some of which are quite long and descriptive, it is very likely to be a safe purchase. If the description of the product fits our requirements, we are likely to be happy with our transaction.

The same applies to your Holiday Let. Testimonials from previous guests are a great way to show potential guests that booking a holiday with you is very likely to be a great experience.

The number of positive remarks in the visitors' book that you will have in your Furnished Holiday Let will steadily grow. You can use some of these on your website and on the directories to which you subscribe.

Here is one of the examples that we used on our Rhubarb Cottage website. Rather than type out the testimonial I photographed it in the visitors' book to demonstrate its authenticity.

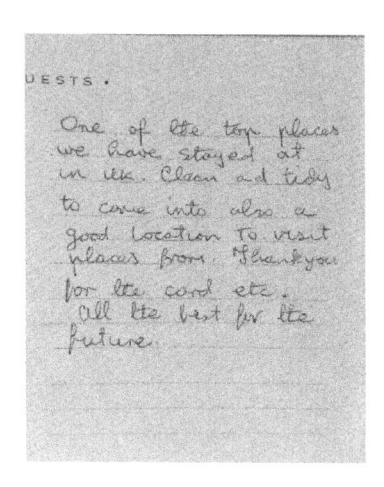

What not to do

In the past at Rhubarb Cottage we have advertised in local papers in different parts of the country, when they have been running a particular promotional theme on tourism or on our local area. We never received a booking from these promotions, so my advice would be – don't bother.

Similarly, there is no need for you to produce a paper brochure for your Furnished Holiday Let. Almost everyone expects to find the details online these days, so a paper brochure is a waste of time and money.

On the odd occasion when we were asked for a brochure by someone who wasn't online, we photocopied 2 or 3 pages from the website and sent those off to the enquirer. We did receive bookings from some of these but we didn't spend any money on printing, just some ink in the computer printer.

Administering your Furnished Holiday Let

You've now set up your Furnished Holiday Let and potential guests have started to see your marketing messages. Perhaps they have searched for accommodation in your area and visited your website. They completed a contact form and ask you a couple of questions about the property and the area. It's important that you reply as quickly as you can. The potential guest may have sent the same enquiry to 3 or 4 different properties. The first one that responds is likely to be in pole position to gain the booking.

Managing a Booking

Let's assume that you responded to the enquiry promptly and the potential guest has agreed to make a booking with you. The guest completes the online booking form which arrives in your inbox.

You will have a number of administration steps to complete:

Update your booking schedule – you will recall from an earlier section that this will show the guest's name, contact number, the week that guest has booked, the number of guests in the party, changeover day, whether or not they are bringing a dog, whether or not they require a cot, highchair, stair gate, anything else and whether they have been before.

Update the booking calendar on your website and any other calendars that you have on directories to which you subscribe. This will block out the week and future guests will not try to book that period. It's important that you do this as soon as possible after you have received the booking.

All of the following will normally be done through email -

Send the guest an invoice for the deposit. This also confirms the booking, with dates, number of guests, total cost and your bank details. Refer your guest to your T&Cs (include a link). This will help if there is any dispute at a later date or a cancellation.

Your guest will pay the deposit, by whichever means you accept.

You will update the original invoice, showing that the invoice has been paid. This will also include the date when the balance is due and becomes the invoice for the balance.

Update your accounts spreadsheet or accounts package to show the deposit payment.

The balance of payment will be due 6 weeks before your guests are due to arrive (or whatever date you set). Your guest will usually pay the balance and send you an email you to tell you that they've paid. If they don't pay by the due date, resend the 'balance' invoice as a reminder and the guest will pay.

> HOW TO SET UP AND RUN A SELF-CATERING
> HOLIDAY PROPERTY

Update your records to show that the Total Balance for the holiday, including any Damage Deposit has been paid.

Update the 'Balance' invoice to show that it is paid and send to your guest.

Update your Accounts spreadsheet or package to show the balance payment.

About 2 weeks before your guests are due to arrive you need to send them directions, how to access the cottage, etc. Ask your guest to confirm that they have received this information – you then know that your guest has the information, in case of any later misunderstandings!

If you have arranged to meet your guests when they arrive, you will need to be at your Furnished Holiday Let well before the agreed time. You should try to be there before your guests arrive.

After the introductions and the guests have gained access to their holiday home, ask them if they have any questions. Answer any that they have and bid a fond farewell. Leave them to settle in and find their bearings.

If you've left the key in a key safe, you will have given your guest the code and they will be able to arrive at any time after the time agreed, which gives them more flexibility and saves you having to attend the arrival at the property.

After the guests have left the property, you will have the changeover to manage (see next section).

Assuming that there is no damage, you will refund the guest's damage deposit. You will need to ask for the guest's bank details to do this. Make the payment through your bank and confirm that you have done this to your guest. This correspondence will also include your thanks to the guest for choosing to stay at your Furnished Holiday Let and good wishes for the future.

Delete the email correspondence with the guest's bank details, so that you comply with GDPR.

Update your Accounts spreadsheet or package to show the damage deposit refund.

Managing Cancellations

Sadly, from time to time, you will have guests who cancel their booking. If the booking was made and payment taken by a directory – TripAdvisor or Airbnb, for example – the directory will manage the cancellation. You won't have to do anything, other than try and re-let the week/weekend that has been cancelled, if there is enough time. Remember that the default cancellation policy on Airbnb will accept cancellations up to the day before the guests were due to arrive, with no financial penalty – it's your money, not theirs…

If you have taken the booking yourself, then you must manage the cancellation. This where your Terms & Conditions will help you. Within your T&Cs you will have a cancellation clause or clauses which cover what your guests can expect in the event of a cancellation.

You might have a clause that looks something like this:

Period before holiday start date when cancellation is notified.	Cancellation charges (% of price)
Up tp 42 days before holiday start date	25%
42 - 21 days	50%
20 - 14 days	60%
13 - 7 days	75%
Less than 6 days before holiday start date	100%

Your guest should be aware of the financial penalty that they will pay when they make the cancellation. Of course, you can choose to override your T&Cs and come to an agreement with your guest. This may well apply if your guest is a regular visitor.

Alternatively, you could have a cancellation clause something like this:

Cancellation - If the hirers have to cancel the holiday, they must notify the owners immediately. The owners will attempt to re-let the property. Until the owners are able to re-let the property for the period of the hire, all balances must be paid, as and when they become due. If the owners cannot re-let the cottage, the hirers will remain liable for the full cost of any part of the holiday that is not re-let. If the owners are able to re-let the hire period, they will refund to the hirers whatever the hirers have paid at that time, less an administration charge of 10% of the total value of the holiday.

This cancellation clause is taken from our Rhubarb Cottage T&Cs (see Appendix 10). Whenever we had a cancellation, we tried to be as fair as possible. In most cases we managed to re-let the cottage and we refunded the guests payments in full.

When you have a cancellation, ensure that you update the guest's invoice to show the cancellation and the amount of the agreed refund.

Transfer the refund to the guest via BACS or other method that you use.

Update your Booking Schedule to free up the cancelled period.

Update your Booking Calendar(s) to free up the cancelled period so that future guests can see that you have a vacancy.

Update your Accounts spreadsheet or package to show the refund.

Since Covid-19 came along, with its associated Lockdowns, both National and Regional, many Furnished

Holiday Lets have introduced a supplementary cancellation clause into their T&Cs. This will look something like this:

Covid-19 additional T&Cs:

1. If you are required to self-isolate while staying at the cottage, you must notify the cottage owners and your entire party must return home immediately. You will not be able to self-isolate at the cottage.

2. If there is a local lockdown in our local area due to Covid19 and the cottage has to close, we will offer you an alternative date of your choice (any price differential to be paid/refunded). The price of the same week next year will not be increased from this year's price.

3. If you become ill with Covid19 or there is a local lockdown in your area and you are not able to take up your booking at the cottage, normal Cancellation T&Cs will apply.

Again, there needs to be some flexibility applied here. Most guests who had their holiday cancelled due to a Covid-19 lockdown were happy to move their booking to later in the year or to the same week the following year, rather than expect a full cash refund from the Furnished Holiday Let owner. In most cases, those who insisted on a cash refund were successful.

Managing your Booking Schedule

There may be times of the year when your Furnished Holiday Let is not available to be booked. As far as possible, you need to plan ahead for this.

You might want to use the property yourself for a holiday and this period needs to be closed in your Booking Calendar(s).

If you are going away for a two week holiday yourself, you either need to close your Booking Calendar(s) for the two weeks so that nobody tries to book those weeks or find someone who can cover the changeovers for you. This comes back to your support network and thinking ahead of all the potential eventualities and issues that you will need to address.

Your Furnished Holiday Let will need to be decorated and updated regularly. You should plan for this in the Low season, when your potential income is at its lowest. Or you can 'play it by ear' and get out the paintbrush in January when you find that you have a week with no booking.

The Changeover

When you run a Furnished Holiday Let, the Changeover, or Turnaround, is absolutely crucial to get right. You are under pressure to do everything that you need to do between your last guests departing and your new guests arriving.

For you, this is another week in the booking schedule. For your guests, this is their holiday which they may have been looking forward to for months. You must keep up your standards and ensure that everything is ready for your guests' arrival. You must do this consistently, week after week, throughout the year. Which means that you (or your employee(s)) have to turn up every week, whether you feel ill or not. Are you up for that?

Planning for the Changeover

By now you will have decided whether to have Friday or Saturday as your changeover day. Whichever day you have chosen, you need to prepare beforehand. You need to make sure that you have enough cleaning materials, including cloths, cleaning sprays of various sorts, sanitising solutions, furniture polish, etc, etc.

You will need to leave some cleaning materials out for your guests, so that they can clean their pots, pans, plates, knives and forks, etc and also wash their clothes. If you have a dishwasher in your Furnished Holiday Let, check that you have enough dishwasher tablets.

Tip: Don't 'skimp' on cleaning materials and buy the cheapest that you can find. Apart from probably not being as effective as the more premium products, if, for example, you leave cheap washing up liquid for your guests to use, this will project an extremely poor image of your Furnished Holiday Let. Your guests will assume that you use 'cheap everything' and they are unlikely to be impressed (and they are unlikely to return).

Bin bags also need to be provided, even if your local authority uses wheelie bins. Waste bins should be provided in all bathrooms/toilets, in the kitchen and in the main rooms. It's a good idea to put a bin liner in these, to make cleaning easier.

Recycling also needs to be encouraged. Leave separate bags in the kitchen for recycling and have a notice highlighting what can and cannot be recycled in your area.

A suggested notice can be seen at Appendix 1.

All of these things and more need to be available to you during your Changeover. If you run out of something important, you may need to go to the nearest shop and buy a replacement, which takes valuable time out of your Changeover hours.

It's a good idea to bulk buy these cleaning materials so that you have a stock of everything. You can keep some of this in a locked cupboard in your Furnished Holiday Let and the rest at your home. At every Changeover, check the stocks of everything at the property and make a list of items that you need to bring with you the following week to replenish your stocks.

You can buy your cleaning materials at any supermarket or order online. Most of the things that you'll need are available on Amazon, which is handy if you need something 'tomorrow'. Lidl and Aldi both have an excellent range of cleaning materials at reasonable prices.

We used to buy about £50 worth of cleaning materials at a time. One day we were in the supermarket and had all our shopping on the belt at the checkout. It was all cleaning materials, nothing else. As we were waiting our turn, a voice behind us said 'Your house must be very dirty, or very clean'. A brilliant comment!

Earlier I mentioned that it is good practice to leave a Welcome Pack. If you provide a Welcome Pack, you will need to buy the contents for the pack a day or two before the Changeover. Bread and cakes have short shelf lives, so you can't buy these too far in advance.

I suspect you think that most of this section so far is obvious. Yes, it probably is but it's worth reiterating how important it is to have everything at your fingertips, ready for the Changeover, when you're up against the clock.

Departing Guests

Your guests will have been notified, probably multiple times, that they need to vacate the property by 10am (this is the most common time quoted for guests to leave a Furnished Holiday Let). Most will remember this, some will forget. Some will remember but choose to ignore the deadline.

At Rhubarb Cottage the performance of our departing guests broke down something like this:

> 60% left before 10am
>
> 25% were still in the cottage at 10am but were almost ready to leave
>
> 10% were still in the cottage but still had packing to finish
>
> 5% hadn't even started to pack

When you arrive at your Furnished Holiday Let a few minutes before the 10am deadline, you never quite know what you're going to find. If the guests' car has gone you (usually) know that you can get straight on with the cleaning.

If the guests' car(s) is still parked outside, you have to wait until 10am before you can ring the doorbell. We were quite strict on this, because of the tight Changeover schedule and we always rang the bell at 10.01am. Most guests were lovely people and welcomed us in and left as soon as they could. If they had a lot of packing left to do, we asked them to get all of their belongings out of the bedrooms, so that we could at least start cleaning there and changing the bedclothes.

HOW TO SET UP AND RUN A SELF-CATERING HOLIDAY PROPERTY

The worst episode that we ever had was ringing the bell at 10.01am and finding that the family of six were just sitting down to eat their Full English Breakfast! I couldn't believe that anyone could be quite so selfish with a complete lack of empathy for the holiday home owner (me). I was quite abrupt with them and asked them to eat their breakfast then pack and go. That, of course, meant that we had to do all the (very dirty) washing up but I would rather do that and get them out of the door, than have them hanging around for even longer. Thankfully, they never rebooked!

Sometimes, when you walk in the house feels like a sauna. Your departing guests have turned up the thermostat to make the property warm (hot) safe in the knowledge that they aren't paying the (very high) gas bill!

When you walk through the door of your property (and temporarily reclaim it), it's easy to be a little nervous. Will the guests have left the property looking as if it's never been used? Will it look like the departing guests ran round with the vacuum cleaner at the last minute when actually, it's a bit of a mess? Worse still, will the guests have walked out leaving plates on the table, rubbish overflowing in the bins and dog poo in the garden? For us, the last option was quite rare but happened on occasions, nevertheless.

Who would leave your property in such a state? The same people who think it's acceptable to leave their litter lying around when they go to the park for a picnic or who throw their rubbish out of the car window, I expect.

Getting on with it

Once your guests have departed, or are almost out of the door, it's a good idea to have a quick walk around the property and assess how it's been left. Sometimes, you'll be pleasantly surprised and your Furnished Holiday Let looks like it's been left ready for the next guests. This is unusual, sadly.

More usually, in our experience, your departing guests will leave the property tidy and superficially clean. Not clean enough to excuse you from cleaning the place from top to bottom though!

You will also want to have a quick look in the Visitors' Book to see if your departing guests have left any comments, preferably positive ones!

If you employ a cleaner, then they will know what to do and get stuck in. You will either help out by doing some of the cleaning, particularly if it's a larger property, or you might oversee things and check to make sure that everything is running as it should.

Your departing guests will have left plenty of rubbish, both general waste and recycling. You will need to take that away, you can't leave it until the dustman comes; your new guests wouldn't be impressed.

Check your inventory and replace any missing, chipped or cracked items. Inspect bedding and soft furnishings for tears in the fabric. Check that light fittings and bulbs are all working and replace if necessary. Check for loose toilet

HOW TO SET UP AND RUN A SELF-CATERING
HOLIDAY PROPERTY

seats and window handles. Make sure that the oven works. Touch up any scuffs or marks on the paintwork (using the paint and brush that you keep at the property for just such an eventuality). Turn down the thermostat to an appropriate setting (depending on the season). Etc, etc.

Most Furnished Holiday Lets will have outside space and this must be kept looking clean and tidy. A lawn will need mowing, flower beds will need weeding and planting. This will also need a good watering in the warmer months. A garden shed or summerhouse will need repainting every year. Etc, etc.

It's a good idea to draw up a cleaning and maintenance checklist. You might see this as overkill, but it's especially useful if you need to employ a new cleaner or if your cleaner lets you down and you find that you've got to do everything yourself.

It isn't possible to 'deep clean' every room every week, there just isn't enough time. The bathroom(s) and kitchen do need to be thoroughly cleaned each week. At Rhubarb Cottage, we got into a rhythm of deep cleaning one room every week. All of the furniture was moved and everything was cleaned, dusted and polished. If you have six rooms, excluding kitchen and bathroom(s), then each room will be deep cleaned every six weeks.

Every room was thoroughly cleaned every week, of course, but every six weeks, the skirting boards behind the wardrobes were polished too!

You do need to make sure that you keep up your cleaning regime. This is particularly important since Covid-19 has come along. Cleanliness and sanitisation are more important than ever. You need to ensure that your guests feel safe in your Furnished Holiday Let. A scrupulously clean property will make even the most nervous guest feel more comfortable.

Providing you carry out your cleaning regime to a high standard, the vast majority of your guests will be quite happy. There will always be a few, though, who are much more difficult to please.

There was a programme on TV a few years ago called 'Four in a Bed'. Four couples who all ran their own Bed & Breakfast businesses, took it in turn to host the other three couples in their B&B. The three couples were encouraged to find fault with the host's property and customer service skills. Viewers would regularly see the guests running their hands along the top of picture frames to check for dust, lifting the bath plug to look for stray hairs and checking the best before dates on boxes of breakfast cereal. And worse ...

It was an entertaining programme and most criticism was taken as 'constructive', though some of the couples fell out over fairly trivial 'observations' (and some not so trivial ...).

You can probably still see reruns of the programme on Dave!

I'm telling you about Four in a Bed because, at some point, you will have guests who would be perfect candidates to appear on the programme. A guest who falls into this category may check for dust on the top of the picture frames and on the top of wardrobes. They will certainly check for hairs in the shower waste and inspect the carpets for specks of dirt.

Very often, these guests suffer from OCD (Obsessive Compulsive Disorder) and there is nothing that you can do, other than ensure that your Furnished Holiday Let is as clean is it could be.

Other guests who find fault in this way are just looking for a reason for you to give them a price reduction! If somebody complains and the complaint is justified, then a small reduction in the agreed price might be appropriate. If it's a ploy to get you to reduce your price for something that's really trivial, you can argue the point. You could offer them a discount on a return visit (in the knowledge that they are unlikely to return).

If you allow dogs to stay in your Furnished Holiday Let you need to be aware that they can leave a smell in the property. Most dogs don't, but some do.

When you vacuum clean the carpets and floors you might be picking up dog hairs and these might smell. As you vacuum, you will be spreading the smell around the property. Non dog owners, in particular, might pick up this smell when they arrive for their holiday. It's good practice to use vacuum cleaner scent tablets or scented filter patches in your vacuum cleaner at all times, to eliminate the doggie smell. Apparently, cinnamon also works, though we've never tried it.

When you have finished your cleaning, you will, obviously, leave the vacuum cleaner emptied and cleaned, for your guests to use as they wish. If your new guests have a dog, add the scented tablet or patch to your vacuum cleaner.

As previously mentioned, at Rhubarb Cottage we left a Welcome Pack for our guests. This needed to be set up as part of the changeover process. We put milk, butter and a bottle of white wine in the fridge. We had a wooden tray on which we placed a quality seeded loaf of bread and if the new guests were bringing a dog, we added a packet of dog chews. In a bowl, we made a nest of straw or tissue paper and placed six free range eggs on top. We then added the bowl of eggs to the wooden tray, with the loaf of bread. We left this on the kitchen worktop.

We also arranged a vase of seasonal flowers on the dining table together with a Welcome card for our new guests.

Your precious few hours of changeover time are also the best time to meet any of your support network who need to carry out routine maintenance. Perhaps the boiler needs a service or the oven or the windows need to be cleaned. If you employ a gardener, they will be turning up on changeover day as well. So, it's a busy time!

When you've finished your cleaning, inside and out, walk around the property and imagine that you have just arrived for your holiday. Are you happy with what you see? If not, sort out the issue.

Check any special requirements that the guests have requested – do they need a baby's highchair or cot, for example? If so, are they set up for the guests?

Now you're ready for your guests to arrive.

First Impressions

We all know that first impressions count. This is certainly true for your Furnished Holiday Let. The first impression that your arriving guests have is crucial. This starts when your guests arrive – your 'kerb appeal' must send the right messages (even if you don't have a kerb outside of your property).

The area at the front should be clean and tidy. Hanging baskets always make a nice impression, as do a clean driveway and nicely tended flower beds. Even if you don't have any space at the front of your Furnished Holiday Let, make sure that the windows are clean, the window frames are cleaned of spiders' webs and bird poo and the door furniture on the front door has been polished.

Have you compiled that cleaning checklist? Don't forget the front of the house, to ensure that there is no reason for your guests' first impressions to be negative.

If you meet your guests when they arrive you will let them into the property and probably into the main living room. You'll answer any questions that they have and then leave them to it. If your changeover has been carried out properly, they are unlikely to be disappointed.

When you have a 'key safe' for the key with a combination lock, you won't see your guests when they arrive. They will let themselves in (providing they have remembered the combination of the key safe) and have that all important first impression of the interior of your Furnished Holiday Let. Once again, if you've done your job, they're likely to be impressed and settle in happily, particularly when they find the bottle of wine in the fridge!

After your guests depart

The changeover isn't complete when you leave your new guests to enjoy their holiday. Your vehicle (or your cleaner's vehicle) will be loaded up with the rubbish left by the departing guests and the bedding, towels, kitchen towels, etc that have been used.

The rubbish needs to be disposed of, either at your local council tip or taken to your home to be collected by your local dustmen.

The bedding and towels need to be washed, dried, ironed and aired, ready to be used in the future.

Any issues that you have discovered during the changeover need to be addressed. Brocken crockery replaced, cleaning materials to be replaced, new batteries purchased, etc.

It's all go, running a Furnished Holiday Let

What could possibly go wrong?

Now you've set up your Furnished Holiday Let and you've had your first few happy guests. It all seems very straightforward once you get into the routine of it all.

Whilst very little will go wrong most of the time, there will be occasions when your patience and ingenuity are stretched to the limit.

As I have already stressed a couple of times, there is only a very short time period between your previous week's guests leaving and the time that the next guests arrive - 4 or 5 hours. So, if anything out of the ordinary happens at this time, you're up against it to get everything ready for your new arrivals. That's why something that you would normally take in your stride can cause a certain amount of stress.

Walking into the property at 10am to find a broken toilet seat, for example, is far from ideal. If you have time, you can drive to the toilet seat shop (B&Q?), purchase the new seat, (if it's in stock) drive back and fit it (assuming that the seat that you have purchased fits your toilet). Your new guests will never know.

Alternatively, you could leave a note for the new guests, explaining what has happened and reassuring them that you will resolve the problem as soon as possible. Not ideal, but most people will understand.

If you've had to do all of that on your own, with no cleaner, you will really be struggling to complete the changeover before the next guests arrive. That is one reason why I would suggest that you always have some help, either every week to help with the cleaning or 'on call' in case of emergencies.

What I would say at this point is that most guests are very understanding. If you do find yourself with a problem at the property when the guests arrive, throw yourself on their mercy. Explain the situation and that you will get it resolved. Most guests will be very accommodating and might even arrange to be in when a tradesman calls to fix something.

If you're really lucky, one of your guests might be a tradesman who can fix the problem for you!

So, what sort of things could throw you off balance? What follows are some examples of what can go wrong. Most of these are unlikely but could happen. It's as well to be aware of these issues, even if you can't plan for them. You should at least give some thought to what you would do, if any of these issues occur in your Furnished Holiday Let.

In no particular order –

Your cleaner doesn't turn up

If you are running your holiday cottage yourself, you will probably employ a cleaner.

(TIP: It's a very good idea to budget for a cleaner. Apart from anything else, it means that if something does go wrong, you have more time to sort out the issue while the cleaner carries on with the cleaning).

Most weeks, even if you have a cleaner, you will visit the cottage yourself, to make sure that everything is OK and to help out, if there is a lot to do. If your cleaner doesn't turn up you have two options:

Find someone else to stand in at short notice

Do it yourself

The first option is worth planning for. If you can arrange for a friend or relative to stand in at short notice they can, at least, help you with the cleaning. They might only be able to give you two hours but that assistance can be invaluable.

If you have to do everything yourself, then you need to get stuck in and prioritise what you do. If you're lucky, your previous guests will have left the cottage very clean and tidy, in which case you will be able to manage the turnaround easily. If the cottage is left in a mess, you may need to prioritise what you do. Change the bedding, pay scrupulous attention to bathrooms and the kitchen but leave the dusting until last. If you're running out of time, dust the main furniture and vacuum the main areas. Make a note for next week to pay particular attention to any areas that you had to leave.

Your cleaner probably has a very good reason for letting you down. If, though, this becomes a regular occurrence, you may need to part company.

You are ill and can't do the Changeover

Managing a Furnished Holiday Let is a tie if you are managing everything yourself. You have to be available and 'raring to go' every Friday or Saturday, depending on your changeover day. Some weeks you will also need to be available during a day in midweek, when you have a 'part week' booking.

We all fall ill from time to time and if you are 'under the weather' on a changeover day and can't manage to do the work you will need to have some backup. If you employ a cleaner, they will be able to cover for you. They may need to prioritise what they do in the time available, but they will get through.

If you don't have any backup, you are in trouble! Your partner, member of your family or a friend might be suitable and amenable to helping out in a crisis.

You must plan for this eventuality as it is almost certain to occur at some point. This should be considered as part of your 'support network'.

The cottage resembles the Marie Celeste

Most departing guests will leave the cottage fairly clean and tidy with pans and dishes washed and stacked away, the carpets vacuumed, and the beds tidied. Others will leave the cottage cleaner and tidier than when they arrived – you hope that they rebook every year!

Sometimes, though, you will walk into the cottage to be greeted by a scene resembling the Marie Celeste. There will be plates left on the table, some with partially eaten breakfast slowly congealing around the cutlery. The kitchen sink will be full of pots and pans. The oven will be filthy, the rubbish bin will be overflowing, the TV will be on, showing Saturday Morning Kitchen and the back door will be open. You almost expect to see the guests appear and start to clear up. Except, of course, they don't. It's as if they have been abducted by aliens. They have just left everything for you to do. You wouldn't do this when you go on holiday would you. Neither would we. But some people have completely different standards and expectations. All part of life's rich pattern. You just have to roll your sleeves up and get on with it. The clock is ticking. It's at times like this that you will be pleased that you employed a cleaner!

Your departing guests show no sign of being ready to depart at departure time

I used this example earlier but it's worth repeating here as it is something that can go wrong and throw you behind schedule.

Most departing guests will vacate the cottage by the appointed time. Some may be just walking out of the door but you will be able to get inside and start stripping the beds. On occasion, though you will arrive at the vacation time to find your guests still eating their Full English Breakfast ...

They will probably apologise profusely, saying that they didn't realise that they needed to be out by the appointed time (they're probably telling the truth because they haven't bothered to read any of the guidance that you've left them). In this situation, the best response (in our experience) is to be firm and tell them that you need to prepare the cottage for the arriving guests and that you need to start the changeover. Embarrass them into clearing everything out of the upstairs rooms, which means that you can start to sort things out upstairs.

Keep walking past them if they are loitering and don't accept any offers to wash up – at this point you want to get rid of them, not give them something else to do. You'll be resigned to clearing everything up. It's rather like the Marie Celeste example above, except that you've arrived before they've left.

Dog Wee

During the cleaning routine you or your cleaner detect dog wee on the carpet or full length curtains. Dog urine has a particularly acidic smell and anyone with a reasonable sense of smell will notice this immediately. In our experience this is very rare. Dog owners are usually fastidious in ensuring that their dogs leave no trace of having been on holiday.

You need to prepare for this by buying a cleaning agent which you can use on the affected area and which will dry before your next guests arrive. Worst case, your curtains may need to be dry cleaned. If you don't have a spare pair of curtains you will need to take the curtains to the dry cleaners asap and leave a message with the new guests that you will return to hang the cleaned curtains the following day. (Best not to mention the dog wee).

Dog Poo

Guests who bring their dogs on holiday are almost always the cleanest guests. They clean up after their dog(s) and they clean up after themselves. They do not want to tarnish the good name of dog owners and most will go to some length to ensure that, if they would like to return, you will be more than happy to welcome them.

Sometimes an owner can miss a dog poo in the garden, and it is always advisable to check the garden very carefully during the changeover. You don't want your new guests to find a dog poo left over from your previous guests, particularly if it was a large dog (or worse, more than one large dog).

We had an unfortunate incident when we had snow for several days (very unusual in our part of the country) and the garden was covered in layers of snow including on changeover day, the day that our guests departed. The new guests arrived with the garden still covered in snow. The thaw arrived a couple of days later to reveal several piles of dog poo scattered around the garden. Embarrassing, but not a lot we could have done to prevent this. The dog owners must have realised that their dogs had pooed in the garden but couldn't see the evidence under the snow.

The new guests, dog owners themselves, were very understanding.

Flea Infestations

We had an issue some years ago when a party of guests told us that the cottage was infested with fleas. They had red 'bites' on their legs and arms and were convinced that a dog that had stayed at the cottage previously had left its fleas to multiply in the carpets. There were two 'saving graces' from this episode. The first was that the guests phoned to tell us the day before they were leaving, rather than telling us after they'd left. This enabled us to buy 'flea bombs' and flea spray so we were prepared when we arrived for the changeover.

After the guests departed, we sprayed all of the carpets and soft furnishings and set off a 'flea bomb' in the main downstairs area. The 'bomb' sprays flea poison all around the surrounding area. The downside is that the area is unusable for several hours. The second saving grace was that the next guests weren't arriving until the following day, so we had enough time to use the 'flea bomb'. If we hadn't had this grace period, we would have sprayed the furniture and then used the 'flea bomb' when time allowed.

We were never convinced that the fleas every existed. None of our other guests ever mentioned fleas and we never suffered from flea bites. We suspect that the 'bites' experienced by our guests were picked up in the forest rather than in the cottage.

Saved Radio Channels

You probably have a radio in the cottage which has pre-tuned channels. Sometimes you will arrive for the changeover and find that all of the saved channels have been mixed up or lost. This may be because the guests have pulled out the power plug (despite you having taken the trouble to fix a label on the plug saying something like 'Please do not disconnect this plug') or they may have fiddled with the tuning without realising that some channels are pre-tuned.

This is something that can take several minutes to rectify, and you may not be able to spare this time that morning. It all takes time. If you have the time, re-tune the radio stations. If you don't have the time, leave it until another day. Your guests will never know, although you will feel that your presentation isn't as professional as it should be.

Alternatively, buy a Smart Speaker! Not everyone will appreciate talking to 'Alexa', though, and we found that keeping a digital radio in the cottage was a good compromise.

Blood on the bedding

Sometimes guests will have accidents in bed. Usually, they will wash the bedding themselves or tell you that they have stained the sheets. This isn't usually an issue. Blood on the sheets, though, requires more attention. Stain remover needs to be applied to the affected areas and the bedding often needs to be washed two or three times. You will have spare bedding, so blood on the pillow cases or sheets is not really a problem. It is more of a problem if it seeps through onto the pillows or the mattress.

You should use a pillow protector over all pillows and a mattress protector on the mattress. You should also have spares of these so that they can be changed regularly and you should also have a spare on standby for emergencies like blood seepage. If blood does seep through the bedding, the pillows and mattress will be protected.

Carpet Damage

Stains on a carpet are quite common and you will need to have a ready supply of carpet cleaning materials on hand. You can either spray this on the affected areas or you can use a carpet cleaner (like a vacuum cleaner) to treat a larger area. This can usually be managed during the changeover period.

More serious is actual damage to the carpet, which you don't want to find when you arrive for the changeover. This might be a burn or damage to the carpet pile. This can't be resolved during the changeover period and while you may be able to recover some of the costs from the guest's damage deposit (if you have arranged one) you will still be left out of pocket and now be the owner of a damaged carpet.

You will usually be able to disguise the damage by placing a rug over the affected area. If that isn't possible, you will need to explain the situation to your arriving guests, who will almost certainly be very understanding of your predicament. If the carpet is old, then perhaps it needs to be renewed. If it's still in good condition, you could ask a carpet fitter (the one on your 'local support network' list) to come and 'patch in' a new piece of carpet. Not ideal, but it's better than leaving an obviously damaged carpet for your future guests to notice (and criticise …).

Breakages

As you go through the cleaning routine you may find various breakages which your departing guests haven't owned up to. A broken wine glass or a cracked plate. Or you tidy up the cupboard and realise that you've only got 5 wine glasses instead of 6. There may be marks on the paintwork. This can all be classed as 'wear and tear' and you expect this to happen from time to time.

If a more serious breakage occurs you would expect guests to own up and, in our experience, they usually do. You will need to consider whether to deduct the replacement costs from the damage deposit which they will have lodged with you.

If the damage is such that the cost to replace or repair is greater than the damage deposit you will have to sit down with your guests and agree the level of compensation. Most guests will agree to pay. If they don't, you can either shrug your shoulders or tell them that they will be hearing from your insurance company. Your insurance will cover you for the costs, less any excess fee and the company may attempt to recover their costs from your guests.

Some guests will have their own insurance cover, which will pay for the damages. This is the best outcome but, sadly, most people don't take out insurance for holidays unless they go abroad.

The worst incident that we've had involved nail varnish on the polished dining room table. A young girl was putting nail varnish on her nails and accidentally knocked the pot of nail varnish all over the table. This caused a huge mark on the table. The guests were very apologetic, and we kept the damage deposit. I was able to make a pretty good job of polishing out the stain with a mix of mayonnaise and ashes (yes, really!). Thank you Google ...

Since this incident, we cover the table in a plastic tablecloth under a decorative cloth cover. It doesn't look quite as traditional as the bare wood polished table but is much more practical.

Broken vacuum cleaner

You rely on the vacuum cleaner during the changeover period so to arrive at the cottage and find that the vacuum cleaner isn't working, is not what you need. It may be repairable – the filters may be clogged up or you find that the rotating brush at the front is full of hair. These things are not too bad, though they do take up your valuable time to fix.

Worse is when the vacuum cleaner is really kaput and needs to go to the repairer. You can't clean a property without a vacuum cleaner so you will probably have to go back to your house to pick up your own cleaner. Again, this takes time but may be your only alternative.

Once again, this proves the value of employing a cleaner who can be getting on with the changeover while you are doing a run around, fetching a replacement vacuum cleaner, all in the four/five hour time slot between guests.

Cordless vacuum cleaner

We needed to replace the existing plug-in vacuum cleaner and decided to buy a Dyson cordless rechargeable model. This looks more modern and is easier to use.

The vacuum cleaner was always left at the cottage so that our guests could use it (or not). Most guests used it when they did their tidying up before they left.

So far so good.

During the second changeover after we had replaced the vacuum cleaner, the flaw in the plan appeared. Our departing guests has used the Dyson (thank you) and had left it in the cupboard where it was usually stored. Sadly, the battery was now flat! So another trip back to our house to pick up our own vacuum cleaner...

We quickly replaced the cordless Dyson with a plug-in model.

The oven is filthy

Another unwelcome sight when you do the changeover is a filthy oven. Some guests will at least try to clean the oven. Some don't, though. Why are these the families that cook all of their meals from scratch rather than live on takeaways?

There's nothing for it but to roll your sleeves up again and get on with cleaning the racks and the inside of the oven. With a liberal amount of elbow grease you will be able to do a pretty good job at cleaning the oven. If there are burn marks and stains that you can't remove, arrange for a commercial oven cleaning company to clean the oven during the next changeover period. They will be able to achieve this in the four hour window and your oven will sparkle with a new lease of life.

(Tip: Keep a range of cleaners at the cottage, locked away from any children's' prying hands. This will enable you to clean up most spills and marks without having to rush out to the shop during the changeover).

Blocked drains

Blocked drains should be a rare occurrence but is something that you should be prepared for. Keep a set of drain rods in your garage for emergencies. If you have time, you can call Dyno-Rod or one of the other drain clearance companies who will sort out your problem. If though, your next guests are arriving in four hours' time, you might want to try to remove the blockage yourself.

Often, it's just a case of lifting up a manhole and poking the drain rods down to move the obstruction.

If it's something more dramatic, then call the professionals and explain the situation to your guests when they arrive. Most people are very tolerant. If it's a real inconvenience, then you may need to consider some form of compensation, to smooth things over.

The Toilet won't flush

Like blocked drains, this can be a difficult situation to fix in the limited time between turnarounds. If the flushing mechanism is broken, you could go to B&Q (or similar), buy a new one and fit it yourself. But what if you aren't an amateur plumber?

You will need to go to your list of tradesmen (and women) and throw yourself on the mercy of your plumber. They may be able to come out at short notice and fix the issue before your next guests arrive. More likely, you will need to book the plumber to come out as soon as they can. If you have more than one toilet, you can explain what's happened to the guests and hope they understand – most will.

If you only have one toilet, then time is of the essence. Your best bet is to contact a 24 hour plumber who can come out quickly. This is likely to be very expensive, but needs must! Compensation for your guests may be appropriate here too, depending on how high the temperature rises.

Theft

As I've explained earlier, our cottage was in in road called The Custards, so our Furnished Holiday Let was 'Rhubarb Cottage in The Custards'.

Inside the cottage we had various bits and pieces that related to Rhubarb or Custard. Among these was a bottle of Rhubarb Wine, which was displayed on a rack on the sideboard.

One day we arrived at the cottage on Saturday morning to find that the bottle was missing. The previous guests had taken it home with them. We contacted the guests, who quite brazenly said that they thought the bottle was for them to take away as a souvenir. Grrr.

Bottles of Rhubarb Wine are not easy to come by. When we've seen them for sale online, the post and packing has been more expensive than the wine! We eventually found another one in a gift shop. We hung a notice around the neck of the bottle saying, 'For Display Only'.

That bottle lasted about two years before somebody drank it and left the empty bottle behind.

One of our regular guests then very kindly bought us another bottle of Rhubarb Wine. She suggested that we drink the wine ourselves, put coloured water (or something worse) back in the bottle and reseal it. We didn't take her advice on that, though we were tempted.

Some people seem to expect to be able to take things home with them. We've lost count of the number of clothes hangers that we've lost and several towels have mysteriously disappeared.

Renovations next door

Rhubarb Cottage is a semi-detached Victorian cottage. Some years ago, the adjoining half was sold and the new owners completely renovated the property before they moved in, a process that lasted about six months. We were concerned about noise, but the neighbours were very good and agreed that the builders wouldn't start work before 8.30am.

Work started and progressed on schedule. There was inevitably some noise and an unsightly skip outside and we did warn all of our guests what to expect. Everything went well until the roof was replaced. The old, tiled roof was taken off, slate by slate and new wooden batons were fixed in place while a temporary tarpaulin covered the roof to protect the cottage from the elements.

Then the slates were refitted onto the new batons, one by one. This involved tapping nails into each slate, one at each top corner. You can imagine that took some time.

As agreed, the builders didn't start work until 8.30am. But at 8.31am they did start to refit the slates. Tap, tap, tap. Tap, tap, tap. Tap, tap, tap. Tap, tap, tap. On and on and on.

Our guests were still lying in bed at 8.30am (fair enough when you're on holiday) and the continuous tapping became too much for them to bear. It must have seemed like water torture ...

We received a very irate phone call, demanding that we come to the cottage to tell our guests what we planned to do about the situation. What could we do? The neighbours needed to finish their roof and our guests wanted a restful holiday.

We turned up at the cottage and received a real dressing down from the father of the family. We took our punishment, meekly pointing out that we had told our guests that the next door property was being refurbished.

'Yes, and you also said that we wouldn't be inconvenienced', shot back the reply.

We had to take it on the chin in this instance and offered a refund on the holiday which amounted to about 25% of total holiday cost. This brought a broad smile to father and mother's faces and suddenly the tap, tap, tapping wasn't such an issue.

The roof tiling lasted one more day, after which there were no more 8.31am disturbances.

Noisy next door neighbours

If you have a detached property, your guests are unlikely to be disturbed by your neighbours while they are inside the house. If you have a semi-detached or terraced property though, your guests may hear the neighbours through the party wall. This is rarely an issue but can be if your neighbours are particularly noisy. It can also be concerning for your guests if, for example, your neighbours have a dog that continually barks during the day. Your guests may be worried about the dog, and this will undoubtedly affect their holiday, even if the neighbour's dog is perfectly OK.

Your neighbour's family may also make a lot of noise in the garden, particularly young children. A trampoline being erected on next door's lawn is a sure sign of shrieking children coming over the horizon.

This is a tricky situation. You could respectfully ask the neighbour to make less noise, but this isn't likely to be received in the spirit that you intended. You are likely to annoy your neighbour. Don't blame them or accuse them and don't threaten them either – you're trying to find a solution, not start a fight.

It is quite possible that your neighbour doesn't realise that the party wall is so thin. You could broach the subject of the noise bothering you and your guests but be careful not to offend them. You could introduce the subject by saying something like, 'I'm not sure if you're aware, but the walls are really thin here so we can hear quite a lot next door. Do you hear noise from our side?'

You could ask the neighbour if their dog is OK and if there is anything that you can do to help. If they ask why, you could say that your guests mentioned to you that they were concerned about the dog; this might make the neighbour think.

You could also speak to other neighbours, if you know them, to ask if they are being disturbed and if they might mention this to your neighbour. This can be a very effective way to proceed if one of your other neighbours is on friendly terms with the noise makers.

It really depends on your neighbours and your relationship with them. If they are amenable, the noise level may diminish, particularly if it's the children making the noise. If they are not so amenable and they are really noisy, you may need to go down the route of writing a formal letter or, in the worst case, getting the local authority or the police involved. You really need to avoid this, if at all possible.

Guests are noisy

The opposite side of the coin to noisy neighbours is noisy guests. It will be rare for your guests to be noisy unless you decide to specialise in stag and hen parties (not recommended). The vast majority of guests are well behaved and conscious of not upsetting the neighbours. You may have guests, though, who leave their dog(s) in your property unattended for a period of time (even though your terms and conditions might stipulate that no dogs should be left in the property unattended). If the dogs haven't become accustomed to their surroundings they may bark. And bark and bark. Your neighbours may hear this and either be annoyed by the continual barking or concerned for the welfare of the animals, or both.

The dog will soon settle down in its new surroundings so this should be a short-term issue.

More serious would be a noisy family or group who let their hair down a little too far on holiday and stay up late, getting ever rowdier as the night progresses. This may well result in a phone call from the neighbours, and you will need to eat humble pie as the injured party tell you what they think of your holidaymakers.

You will then need to speak to your guests to ensure that they don't upset the local equilibrium again.

There are Apps available which you can download to your mobile phone which will monitor noise levels in your Furnished Holiday Let. You would receive a message if noise levels got too high, which might indicate that a party is going on. You would be able to 'nip things in the bud' before things got out of hand.

Noiseaware is worth looking at if you are concerned about parties:

https://noiseaware.com/

Another App is Party Squasher:

https://www.partysquasher.com/

This is a low cost, easy-to-use solution designed for owners of Furnished Holiday Lets who want to be alerted to any large gathering at a property. Party Squasher prevents parties before the noise starts by continuously monitoring the number of guests at a property.

You would connect a compact sensor to the internet router in your property and Party Squasher counts the number of mobile phones in and around your house. You can view real time guest occupancy anytime on the App.

You set an occupancy limit and you would receive a text message or email when the occupancy exceeds your threshold. Then you can call the guests or take other action.

Noisy guests can also become an issue for the neighbours if you do a lot of very short lets – 1 or 2 nights at a time. This is the 'bread and butter' market of Airbnb. A high percentage of Airbnb bookers book for short stays and 1 or 2 nights is very common. These booking are often made by people who are touring the country and want to see the local sights, then move on to their next destination. Many of these will be foreign tourists. If you have a lot of shorts lets like this, some of your short term guests will arrive at all times of the day (and night), depending on when their train or coach arrives. They are unlikely to be particularly quiet when they arrive, and this can be annoying to your neighbours. If this is a regular occurrence, you will soon have an angry neighbour knocking on your door on changeover day.

These short lets should really be left to people who hire out one of their spare bedrooms. It is not the best market for a professional Furnished Holiday Let business.

People with disabilities who you weren't expecting

You may have adapted your cottage to facilitate disabled guests. This might range from grab handles next

> HOW TO SET UP AND RUN A SELF-CATERING
> HOLIDAY PROPERTY

to the toilet and bath to a walk-in shower, low level basin and wheelchair access. You will have prepared your access statement so your guests should know what to expect.

Occasionally you may find that a party with a disabled guest books the cottage without telling you that one of their group is disabled. Depending on the disability, this will be nothing to worry about or a big issue. It's extremely unlikely that a seriously disabled person will book your accommodation without first checking that it is suitable. It is more likely that someone who is mildly disabled – often an older person – comes on holiday with their family. They may not be able to manage to step into the bath, for example, or to stand up after using the toilet.

You can overcome this by fitting grab handles in appropriate places. This will be appreciated by those who need the assistance and will also show that you have thought about people who are less mobile. It will head off any potential complaints which you don't expect and don't need.

A few pounds well spent.

Guests who lock themselves out

Most modern front doors can be secured (but not necessarily locked) by lifting up the handle. It's quite easy, then, for your guests to lock themselves out. They lift the handle, then remember that they've left the key indoors. So, they will phone you up to ask them to let them back in. In this situation it's always advisable to take two spare keys with you – one for the front door and one for another door, the back door or a patio door. This is because, quite frequently, the guest has not only locked themselves out, but they have also left the front door key in the door lock, on the inside. You can't insert your spare key into the front door lock if there is already a key in the lock. Taking another key ensures that you can let your guests back in and you can also retrieve the front door key while you're inside.

This situation is not as rare as you might think!

Front door lock broken or jammed

Another potential problem with the front door is the lock jamming. If the lock jams while the door is closed, that's not too bad. You can ask your guests to use a different door until the front door lock in unjammed. If the front door lock jams while it is open, this is a disaster. The property can't be made safe until the door can be closed. Your only recourse here is to contact an emergency locksmith (the one of your support network list …) and wait until he/she arrives. While you're waiting, you can fiddle with the lock, trying different door handle and key positions, in an attempt to free it. If you are very lucky, the door lock will miraculously free itself and you will breathe a huge sigh of relief.

This has happened to us twice.

Bricks down the chimney – most cottages have issues

Most holiday cottages were built some time ago, often more than a century ago. Inevitably, this leads to deterioration in the fabric of the building, and it can be a constant battle to keep up with repairs. More positively, many cottages have been renovated and ongoing costs will be much reduced. Not every potential problem is immediately visible though.

One evening at Rhubarb Cottage, our guests were quietly enjoying a programme on the TV when a large 'thump' made them jump. Dust suddenly started billowing out of the fireplace, settling on the fire surround and the carpet. On closer inspection, our guests discovered that two whole bricks and several pieces of rubble had fallen down the chimney. This became the talking point of their holiday (and when they returned the following year).

We had an inspection carried out by a specialist with a camera that went up the chimney. This showed that the bricks and rubble had been dislodged not far above the fireplace so not as serious as we first though but still an expensive repair. We decided that, in addition to having the repairs carried out, we would fit a log burner and flue at the same time. We had been considering installing a log burner for so ted us into spending the

> HOW TO SET UP AND RUN A SELF-CATERING
> HOLIDAY PROPERTY

Smoke Alarm batteries run out

As highlighted in an earlier section, a Furnished Holiday Let, like other rental properties, must have smoke alarms on each floor which are connected to the mains electrical supply. Each unit will also have a battery in it, to ensure that the alarm still works in the event of a power outage.

When these batteries start to run down, the alarm emits a bleep. A bleep every 15 seconds or so. After a time, this can also feel a little like water torture – a constant bleep rather than a constant drip.

Understandably, your guests could do without this distraction and you will soon be contacted and asked to stop the bleeping. A new battery will solve the problem. It's good practice to change the batteries in all of the smoke alarm units at the same time, as they will all start to run down at some point.

Even better is to make a calendar note to change all the batteries once a year. This should ensure that your guests are never disturbed by battery bleeping. You should also keep spare batteries locked away at your Furnished Holiday Let, so that they are available when required.

Your guests get lost

We once had a phone call from the local police asking if we were the owners of a cottage called Rhubarb Cottage in The Custards.

'Yes, we are. Why do you ask?'

'We've got a couple here who say that they are staying at Rhubarb Cottage, but they don't know how to get there and they don't know where they've left their car'.

The couple in question and their grown up daughter were staying in the cottage for a week and had driven to Lymington. They couldn't find anywhere to park, so the husband dropped his wife and daughter off at the shops and drove off to find a parking place.

Whilst shopping, the mother lost a glove. The daughter went back to look for it, leaving her mother standing alone.

A young voluntary police officer appeared and asked the mother if she was OK, as she looked lost.

The mother explained the situation and added that she didn't know where the car was parked and she couldn't remember the name of the car or the numberplate, as they had only recently bought the car.

The police officer asked the mother where she was staying, and she replied 'Rhubarb Cottage in The Custards'. This raised some concerns with the police officer, who began to think that the elderly mother was 'losing the plot' (so the mother told us later).

This led to the phone call to us. Our confirmation that the family were, indeed, staying at 'Rhubarb Cottage in The Custards' saved the mother from being 'escorted' to the police station.

> HOW TO SET UP AND RUN A SELF-CATERING
> HOLIDAY PROPERTY

Their car and husband were eventually located, with the help of the police and they were directed back to the cottage at the address that we had confirmed during the phone call.

Needless to say, our guests were very embarrassed about the whole incident, but it became a bit of a standing joke each time they rebooked to stay at the cottage.

The Boiler breaks down

If your boiler is going to break down, you can be sure that it will break down in the middle of winter. This is no coincidence, as your boiler will be working harder in the winter months and any parts that are on the verge of failing will be pushed over the edge by the extra workload.

You won't be alone, of course, as many other boilers will also break down in the winter months. You will have trouble finding a plumber to attend at short notice unless you pay an arm and a leg to an emergency plumber.

Having guests in your cottage with no heating is a disaster that you must try to avoid at all costs. There are several ways that you can be prepared:

> Make sure that your boiler is in good working order. If it's more than 10 years old it is very likely to break down. You should consider replacing it.

If you have a system with a hot water cylinder, make sure that you have an electric emersion heater. This can be used to heat the water if the boiler fails. At least your guests will have hot water.

Take out central heating/boiler breakdown cover with a reputable supplier. This will include an annual boiler service.

If you don't take out breakdown cover, at least ensure that your boiler is serviced annually. This should identify any parts that need to be replaced and will reduce the chances of a boiler breakdown.

Buy some electric radiators which can be used in an emergency. The whole house may not be heated by these, but the main rooms can be kept warm and your guests will know that you are doing your best to make them comfortable.

Get to know 1 or 2 local plumbers and add them to your support network. If you have someone that you can call on in an emergency, you have a fighting chance of getting the boiler working again in a short period of time.

If you hear the boiler making an odd noise, or if one of your guests mentions that the boiler is noisy, don't ignore the warning signs. Arrange for a plumber to come during the changeover period and rectify the fault. Better to be safe than sorry.

Power cut

Just as your boiler is important to your guests' wellbeing, so too is your power supply. You must have contingency plans in place to cope if you have a power cut. If the electricity is cut off there is very little that you can do to speed up the restoration of the service. The power transmission company will be working very hard to restore your service, all you can do is make sure that your guests are as comfortable as possible.

Leave a torch (with a working battery) at the cottage. Better still, leave two. Even better, have a wind-up torch in case of a power cut and battery failure!

Have a supply of tealight candles and matches available. (Some people frown on the use of candles because of the danger of setting fire to the property. Tealights will not fall over and are the safest candle option)

If you have a log burner, your guests can at least keep warm. It can be quite pleasant to sit in front of a candle-lit hearth, as long as it doesn't last too long ...

The bed breaks

One morning we received an irate phone call from the guests at the cottage telling us that the bed had collapsed and demanding to know what we were going to do about it. The bed in question was a sturdy metal framed bed but obviously not sturdy enough.

I drove over to the cottage straightaway, wondering how this could have happened and rang the doorbell. My question was answered when the outline of a huge body frame came into view through the frosted glass window in the door. Our guest opened the door to reveal a body that was north of 20 stone and probably growing by the day. His partner stood behind him. She too, was no stranger to the 'All You Can Eat' buffet bar so it was immediately apparent why the bed wasn't up to the job.

Unbelievably, the couple weren't in any way apologetic. They were quite aggressive and annoyed that their holiday had been inconvenienced by the 'inadequate' bed that we had provided.

Never mind that the bed had managed to remain intact over the course of the previous twelve years, with three changes of mattress, it was our fault. And as the customer is always right, it was, indeed, our fault.

I went upstairs to survey the damage. I pulled off the mattress to find that the central metal bar running from top to bottom of the bed under the mattress had bent in the middle. I unscrewed the bar and took it out leaving a large rectangular hole with no support for the mattress. Fortunately, the couple were the only guests staying at the cottage so they were able to move into the spare bedroom while the main bed was being repaired. The second bedroom had a wooden framed divan bed which was more solid and survived the strain under which it was placed.

I took the metal bar to a welder (another trade to add to your 'support network'. We have 'Metal Steve' who is always very helpful when we have a need for his services) who straightened it out and reinforced it with new metal sides and a new leg in the middle of the bar. I took it back to the cottage the following day, refitted it and made up the bed.

Since then, we've had no complaints about the bed. Unsurprisingly, Mr and Mrs Large haven't returned.

A huge gas bill

When you run a Buy to Let property you generally pay the mortgage on the property, but your tenants pick up the 'day to day running' bills – Council Tax, Utilities,

Telephone, etc. This is not the case with a Furnished Holiday Let. You will be picking up all of the bills so, to the holidaymakers, everything is 'free'. Many of your guests won't be shy in turning up the thermostat on the heating as they aren't paying for the gas/electric.

When you turn up for the weekly changeover it sometimes seems as if you are walking into a sauna, not surprising when you see that the thermostat is set at 30 degrees. If you have an online account with your energy provider that shows monthly or weekly usage graphically, you will see large variations in weekly usage. This is, of course, reflected in your energy bill and you should budget for higher bills than would be the case if you were living in the property.

You could invest in Hive or Nest (or similar) which would allow you to adjust the temperature using an App on your mobile phone. I strongly suggest that you don't do this, as some of your guests will think that you are spying on them. They might be right ...

Double booking

This is a disaster that we have narrowly avoided a couple of times. When you take a booking, make sure that you get into the habit of updating your Booking Schedule and online Booking Calendar(s) all at the same time. Don't leave it until some later date to 'do the admin'.

Some holiday directories will automatically accept a booking if the calendar on their site shows availability on the dates requested. If this happens and you have taken a booking elsewhere for the same week, you will need to cancel the later booking which both upsets your 'lost' guests and hurts your stats on the directory site. You will find that your property doesn't rank as highly as it did previously if you cancel bookings. This is particularly true of TripAdvisor.

If you did manage to double book the cottage you would always realise before the date of arrival because you would have two sets of guests paying for the same week. So, you are never going to find yourself in the position of two families turning up on the same day, both expecting to enjoy their holiday in your cottage. You will, though, have a family who you've had to cancel, who are never likely to return and who will probably warn their friends not to book your cottage either.

Keep on top of the admin and avoid this situation at all costs.

Your guests arrive early

You will have written to your guests giving them directions and the time from which they can access the property. This will usually be between 2pm and 4pm on the day of arrival.

The vast majority of your guests will follow your instructions. Some, though, will not read them or forget them, and turn up on your doorstep early. When this happens the inside of your property will look a mess as you will still be cleaning. Your guests will either realise their error and go off to find somewhere for lunch or find a local attraction.

Alternatively, they will ask if they 'could possibly come in early'. This is very awkward, especially if your guests have come from another country and don't speak very good English. In the past we have allowed guests to leave their suitcases in the hallway, so that their car is empty and suggested where they could spend the next couple of hours, or so. This has worked in every case except one. The family were foreign, and their English was basic, at best. I tried to explain to them that they were early, but they just sat down and 'hung around'. In that particular instance we put the TV on (luckily, we had finished cleaning the front room, other than vacuuming) and they were happy.

If that happened today, I would probably try Google Translate to get my message across.

Your guests phone for assistance after you have had a couple of drinks at home

This happened to us once. We had a Saturday changeover and in the middle of the evening the phone rang. It was our new guests. They had managed to lock themselves out and 'could we pop over with a spare key and let them in, please'. Er no, we can't, we've opened a bottle of wine …

HOW TO SET UP AND RUN A SELF-CATERING
HOLIDAY PROPERTY

To overcome this issue, we contacted our cleaner (a teetotaller) who had a key and who very kindly drove over to the cottage to let the guests back in.

It's worth thinking about what you would do, if you found yourself with the same dilemma.

Your guests contact you at an inconvenient time

Most of your guests will never contact you while they are staying in your Furnished Holiday Let. Generally, they will only contact you if they have a problem. The problem could be anything relating to your property, the neighbours, the guests' family, etc.

Most queries can be sorted out over the phone, but some need you to visit the property. This can be very difficult if you are away on holiday yourself! We once had a phone call from a guest while we were on the Rome underground (amazingly, we had a signal).

Once again, you need to plan for this rare eventuality and line up someone to respond in person on your behalf before you go away. Make sure that you have their contact details with you while you are away and leave a key with them, in case of emergencies!

Guest is ill and expects a refund

Your guest contacts you a day before they are due to arrive, to tell you that one of their party is ill and so they won't be coming after all. 'It's such a shame as we were all really looking forward to it. What do we need to do to get our refund?'

Hopefully, your terms and conditions highlight the circumstances when a refund would be appropriate and one day before the arrival date will probably not qualify. Our T&Cs were on our website. Since Covid-19 arrived, we sent a link to the T&Cs to all new enquirers, so that they were clear on our Covid-19 policy. The T&Cs also included our normal cancellation policy and details of the circumstances and timings when a refund would be made.

If you have sent the T&Cs to your potential guests when they booked, they must accept that a refund will not be given if they cancel within a certain time period.

Your recommendations to your guests backfire

In your 'Holiday Guests' Guide' you might recommend local pubs and restaurants to your guests. These will be places where you have had a great experience yourself and/or which have a very good reputation locally. If you allow pets to stay in your Furnished Holiday Let you will probably recommend good local pubs that are dog friendly.

The performance of pubs and restaurants can change over time. Perhaps a new chef arrives (for better or worse) or the business changes hands.

Smaller pubs will have one main chef, often the landlord, and he or she will not work every day, so a second chef will prepare meals on the chef's days off. This may mean that the presentation of the food differs on these days and the customer doesn't receive what they are expecting.

Even worse, one of your guests could go down with food poisoning from food eaten at one of the establishments that you have recommended.

Most of your guests will shrug their shoulders and put their disappointing experience down to 'one of those things'. Some guests, though, will feel that you have a responsibility for their misfortune and expect some form of compensation – you really don't need that!

When you make your recommendations, it is a good idea to add a disclaimer which says something like:

We give you these restaurant and pub recommendations in good faith based on our personal experience. We cannot accept responsibility if the pubs have changed hands or are not as described above due to a change in circumstances – or chefs! If you find that something has changed or would like another recommendation added to this guide, please leave a note for us and we will add it in, for the benefit of future guests.

This is the disclaimer that we used for Rhubarb Cottage and I strongly suggest that you use something similar.

Some guests have a vivid imagination

Your website will tell your potential guests what to expect when they stay in your lovely Furnished Holiday Let. The website will have photographs showing your rooms and your 'personal touches' around the property.

It may come as a surprise, then, when a guest contacts you to ask about something that you don't offer. At Rhubarb Cottage, we had a guest ask how he could access Sky Sports. On our website, we made it quite clear that the Furnished Holiday Let provided a digital TV with Freeview channels. There was no mention of Sky TV, let alone the Sky Sports package.

On the other side of the coin, our website showed pictures of the New Forest ponies on the open forest at the back of our cottage. One of our guests complained that the ponies weren't there, and the children were very disappointed. The ponies are free roaming and wander around the forest at will. Having said that, they don't roam very far from their home territory so our guests wouldn't have had far to walk to see some ponies.

Try and be as precise as you can be when describing what you offer in your Furnished Holiday Let and what your guests can expect.

Overcrowding

It has been known for a party of guests to book for 4 people, then 8 people stay. It's usually obvious when this has happened by the amount of rubbish generated and the number of towels used. We also had guests who didn't declare that they had a dog with them. This was presumably to avoid paying the £25 fee.

On one occasion, the guests had an issue that I needed to sort out which meant that I had to visit the cottage. Imagine my surprise when I was greeted at the front door by two dogs. Two dogs which weren't booked in. It was worth it to see the embarrassment on faces of the dogs' owners – priceless!

There will always be sad people who try to 'pull a fast one' and feel that they have beaten the system. My advice to you, if you get the opportunity, is to make it obvious that you know what they have done but leave it at that. They will always be sad people ...

The weather

One year we had a couple who were both schoolteachers and who booked to stay at Rhubarb Cottage for two weeks in August, during their school holidays. The weather was glorious for the fortnight; the sun shone every day.

They had a lovely time and booked straightaway to come back the following year for the same two weeks in August.

Britain's unpredictable weather lived up to its name. The rain came down every single day of the fortnight. Sadly, they didn't enjoy their return visit quite as much and we didn't see them again.

You obviously can't control the weather. You can though, accept that Britain's weather is never certain and plan for it. Keep a supply of magazines, games, puzzles, DVDs etc in your Furnished Holiday Let so that your guests can amuse themselves when the weather isn't great.

The weather (2)

The weather can be very changeable, particularly in the winter months. This is the season of heavy rain, gales and floods. For this reason, it is also the season when damage to your property is most likely to occur.

At Rhubarb Cottage we have had tiles blown off of the roof and the whole roof of the shed blown away. The worst damage was when an entire length of fencing was blown down, all across the next-door neighbour's garden.

Once again, you can't really plan for this, but you must be aware of what can happen and what you can do about it. In our case, we found a roofer who could replace the lost tiles within a week of them being blown off. I fixed the shed roof back on using the standard multipurpose tools – a hammer and nails...

HOW TO SET UP AND RUN A SELF-CATERING HOLIDAY PROPERTY

The fence was more problematic. Due to the weather, we weren't the only ones who needed new fence panels. New fence panels became hard to find and surprise, surprise when we did find some, the price had gone up quite substantially. Then we had the problem of getting them fitted. All of the fence erectors that we contacted were very busy, so we had to wait over a month for the new fence to be erected.

As this was in January, we didn't have many bookings at the cottage. We contacted the guests that were due to arrive and explained that we didn't have a fence on two sides of the garden. They were very understanding. Luckily, they didn't have a dog, which would have made life much more difficult.

Guests' parking

During the fifteen years that we owned Rhubarb Cottage we only upset the neighbours twice (to our knowledge ...). Both instances were caused by our guests selfishly parking their vehicles in the wrong places.

We had one parking space at the front of the cottage, so one vehicle was always parked there. There was plenty of room in surrounding roads to park a second vehicle and almost everyone who arrived in more than one vehicle found a suitable parking spot.

The first time that we received an angry letter from local residents was when one of our guests parked their second vehicle in front of one of the gates leading into the open forest. This blocked the access for forestry vehicles and emergency vehicles (and any other vehicles). The gate was clearly marked with a 'Please do not park in front of this gate, it is required for emergency access' notice but that didn't seem to matter to our 'entitled' guests. Quite why they thought that it was OK to park their vehicle in front of such a gate is beyond me.

The second time that we caused an upset was when the guests' second vehicle was parked in a road which we had explicitly asked our guests not to park in, because local people needed to park there (see the 'Good Guest Guide' in Appendix 7). Not only did they leave the car in the wrong place, they left it there for six days without using it! Understandably, we were not popular with the neighbours.

As Furnished Holiday Let owners, we must never forget that we don't live in our property, but our neighbours do live in the area. We must ensure that we cause as little inconvenience as possible to everyone living there.

Other 'complaints'

We've all heard stories about people who move to live in the country and then complain that 'the cockerel crowing wakes them up', 'tractors drive too slowly down country lanes', 'farm animals smell', etc.

> **HOW TO SET UP AND RUN A SELF-CATERING HOLIDAY PROPERTY**

Some guests that come to stay in your lovely holiday cottage in the country may have similar issues. We have heard about guests who:

Asked what time breakfast is being served (in a self-catering property).

Asked for a romantic fire to be lit in the property before they arrived. What was intended as a romantic gesture would certainly violate the property's insurance policy, so the request had to be politely declined.

Booked to stay in a farm cottage, then requested a refund because they were scared of the chickens that had free range in the farmyard.

Complained about owls hooting at night, keeping them awake.

Etc, Etc

The list of 'things that can go wrong' is long enough without me pointing out that it is not an exhaustive list. There will be other issues that you come across.

On a positive note, you will not come across many of these issues. You might be fortunate and hardly encounter any of them.

The takeaway from this section is not to scare you into thinking that a Furnished Holiday Let is not for you. The point is that you need to be aware of potential issues and have a plan in place to deal with them, even if it's only a sketchy plan.

Nobody likes nasty surprises. The more that you are prepared, the less nasty these issues will appear.

Nice things about managing a Furnished Holiday Let...

Having given you list of issues that you might encounter, what about the positives of owning a Furnished Holiday Let?

Nice people

While you are running your Furnished Holiday Let you will meet some lovely people. Typically, those who choose to take their holidays in a self-catering property are not intent on having a wild time, out on the town every night until the 'wee small hours'. They are much more likely to be looking for a peaceful, interesting, stress free holiday. A break from the usual routine.

The majority of your guests will be families, of all ages, with or without children. How this splits up for you will depend on your target market, of course.

You will build up a repartee with most guests as you exchange emails or phone calls during the enquiry and booking process. Some of your guests will want to know about the area if it's their first visit. Some will have relatives in the area, some will be returning to their roots, having lived in the area previously.

If you are a nice person (and I'm sure you are), the vast majority of your guests will respond in kind and you will enjoy meeting them.

Returning guests

It's always nice when guests book up for a return visit. You can be sure that they enjoyed staying in your Furnished Holiday Let previously. I mentioned in an earlier section about making notes on guests, particularly anything out of the ordinary. If that guest returns, you can remind them of the incident (unless of course it was a negative point, in which case you won't mention it, but you will be aware of 'what happened last time').

Sometimes returning guests will bring you a present, which is a lovely gesture.

If there is a new local attraction or a new restaurant that has opened since their previous visit, you can draw their attention to it – they will be pleased that you took the time to mention it.

Positive comments

It is always rewarding when your guests leave a nice comment in the visitors' book. Not all your guests will do this and, if they don't, you wonder whether they did enjoy themselves or if you could have done something more for them. When you contact them to return their damage deposit, ask them if all was OK. In most cases you will find that they didn't write anything in the visitors' book because they were too busy packing to meet your deadline for them to leave!

A minority of your guests will also take the trouble to write a testimonial on TripAdvisor or another directory. This will normally be a 4 or 5 star review. Ensure that you answer every testimonial, not only to thank the person who has taken the trouble to write it but also to show other potential guests that you care!

People generally write testimonials because they were very happy with the experience, or very unhappy.

If you receive a 1 or 2 star testimonial your response is critical. If the comments in the testimonial are untrue, say so. If they are exaggerated, say so. If you can inject some humour into your response, the testimonial might go viral! You will have seen examples of this where a customer has been unhappy with the food or service in a particular restaurant and the restaurant owner has responded in a humorous manner. Done well, this will ensure that almost all readers will be on your side and some will even book to stay with you.

Fortunately for us at Rhubarb Cottage we never had a bad review online. We did have negative feedback from some guests (I have used some examples of this already in this book) but they either left a note on the table for us when they left or contacted us via email or telephone. It was a private conversation, as it should be ...

An income stream

Whether you let out your holiday cottage for a few weeks of the year or you run the property as a full time Furnished Holiday Let, you will generate an income stream. This is not the same as a profit stream, of course, but you would hope that your Incomings exceed your Outgoings, in which case you <u>will</u> generate a profit.

How much profit you make will be down to you and your annual profits will probably increase as the years go by. As time goes on, you will become better at buying the things that you need to run your business. You will know more tradesmen and understand roughly how much their work will cost.

You will become better at pricing the weeks that your Furnished Holiday Let is available for guests to book. This is key. As I have said in an earlier section, it is not a race to fill your booking calendar before your competitors. The winner is the one who makes the most money. In this market, though, almost everyone can be a winner if demand for holiday accommodation in your area exceeds supply — which, in most areas, it will.

A property investment

From a financial point of view, running a Furnished Holiday Let is a property investment. You have purchased the property and decided to finance it, in whole or part, by renting it out to holidaymakers. You can be fairly sure that you will make a profit on your bookings if you rent out enough weeks during the year.

What you can't be sure of is whether the value of your property is going to rise or fall. History tells us that, over time, property in the UK has been a good investment. Prices have risen overall but this masks the short-term peaks and troughs.

HOW TO SET UP AND RUN A SELF-CATERING HOLIDAY PROPERTY

Property pricing is cyclical. Prices never consistently go gradually up or gradually down. They tend to 'tread water', then rise rapidly before falling equally as rapidly before levelling out. The hope is that the rises outweigh the falls and in recent decades that is what has happened.

So, whilst you can assume that the value of your property will rise, you can't take this for granted. You might get the timing wrong – buying at a peak and selling into a trough. Sentiment around property investment may change and property prices might stagnate or fall. Never underestimate the ability of the government to intervene in a situation and make it worse!

This is where your attitude to risk comes in, as I have highlighted earlier. If you are completely risk averse, property investment, whether Buy to Let or Furnished Holiday Let is probably not for you.

Nobody ever made a fortune by being completely risk averse though, so some level of risk is necessary in most aspects of our lives. Do what you feel most comfortable doing.

For those who have some appetite for risk, property has been a very good investment. DYOR - Do your own research!

Checklist

The following is a checklist of points that you need to be aware of, most of which you need to action if you are going to make a success of your Furnished Holiday Let and keep within the law.

Which is the best model for your investment - Buy to Let or Furnished Holiday Let?

Letting requirements of a Furnished Holiday Let

Location, Location, Location

Paying for your Furnished Holiday Let

Income Tax implications

Council Tax or Business Rates?

Capital Gains Tax – Entrepreneur's Relief

Capital Allowances

Seasonal Ebbs and Flows in Your Area

Define your Target Market

Accepting Pets or Not?

Managing Your Furnished Holiday Let – Employ an Agency or Do It Yourself?

Holiday Accommodation Accreditation Schemes

HOW TO SET UP AND RUN A SELF-CATERING HOLIDAY PROPERTY

The (ongoing) Effects of Covid-19

Holiday Let Insurance

Safety Rules and Regulations

GDPR – Data Protection

Have your guests 'opted in' to receive future mailings from you?

Furnishing your Furnished Holiday Let

Administration:

Booking Schedule

Booking Calendar(s)

Managing Bookings

Invoices and Receipts

Managing Cancellations

Guest correspondence and instructions

Setting Pricing – Week by Week

Adjusting Pricing, particularly Late Availability

Tracking Expenditure

Terms and Conditions

Choosing your Changeover Day

Your Support Network

Developing your Website

- Website Hosting
- Linking to Directories
- Choosing a Domain Name(s)
- Using Social Media
- Managing your Changeover
- An Understanding of What Can Go Wrong

In Conclusion

If you are seriously considering running a Furnished Holiday Let, I hope you found this book interesting and informative. It should give you a good basis on which to make your decisions –

> Is a Furnished Holiday Let right for me?
>
> What is the best way to manage my Furnished Holiday Let?
>
> Do I have the time and energy to run it myself?
>
> It is a long-term commitment – am I prepared for that?

Undoubtedly, the easiest way to run a Furnished Holiday Let is by handing it over to an agency to manage and paying them a hefty commission for their time and effort. If you are renting out your own holiday cottage for a few weeks in the year and your cottage is not close to your main residence, it makes sense to ask an agency to do the work for you.

The most profitable way to do it is to run it yourself, but that takes time and is a major commitment.

The choice is yours ...

Thanks for reading the book!

HOW TO SET UP AND RUN A SELF-CATERING HOLIDAY PROPERTY

Appendices

These appendices are included to illustrate specific points in the book. They are examples which you can use as a reference and/or adapt to your own circumstances.

Appendix 1 – an example of recycling instructions for guests, as used in Rhubarb Cottage

Managing Waste

In The New Forest, all waste is either recycled or is used as Biomass, to produce energy. Nothing goes to landfill.

The council is very keen to ensure that all waste that can be recycled is put into the CLEAR plastic bags. Please put the following into the clear plastic bags:

All Paper, except wrapping paper or shredded paper.

All Cardboard, except drinks cartons.

All Food Tins, Drinks Cans, empty Aerosols – please rinse tins first. This excludes aerosols with a black cross or skull and crossbones on them.

All Plastic Bottles – but not the caps.

DO NOT recycle:

Plastic Packaging – e.g. Yoghurt pots, Margarine tubs, Plastic tops.

Shredded Paper.

Gift Wrap.

Drinks Cartons.

Bottles and Jars – these should be left in the plastic crate by the back door.

Waste is collected on **Tuesday**. Please put the rubbish that you've collected by Monday evening in front of the cottage for collection in the normal way.

The remainder of the waste will be sorted out by us after you leave. Waste generated by guests in a Holiday Cottage is classed as Trade Waste, believe it or not. The waste that is not collected on Tuesday has to be transferred, by us, to Trade Waste sacks and we have to pay a fee (per bag) to have this collected.

Can we please ask you to follow these guidelines as we do not want to be fined by the council!

Many Thanks

Rob and Karen

Please, please put your waste out for collection on Tuesday...

HOW TO SET UP AND RUN A SELF-CATERING HOLIDAY PROPERTY

Appendix 2 – an example of a Fire Safety Risk Assessment

Risk Assessment – Record of significant findings

Risk assessment for	Assessment carried out by
Building: Orange House Farm Bed & Breakfast Address: High Lane Any Town AA11 6ZZ	Date: 17/8/08 Completed by: A Smith Signature: A Smith

Floor/area:	Use:
A two storey farmhouse with six bedrooms. Two first floor bedrooms for B&B guests and rest of the farmhouse shared with family	Farmhouse providing bedrooms for bed & breakfast, other facilities shared with family

Step 1 – Fire hazards

Sources of ignition	Sources of fuel	Sources of oxygen
Heat from cooking Smoking materials Tumble dryer	Cooking oils Furniture and bedding Clothes in laundry/tumble dryer area	Cleaning materials (Peroxides in cleaning store)

Step 2 – People at risk

Guests anywhere in the house, including any who are elderly, disabled or very young

Step 3 – Evaluate, remove, reduce and protect from risk

What is the risk?	Risk from cooking no greater than when family alone occupying premises, smoking not allowed by guests, no family members smoke
Who is at risk?	Fire can spread throughout the building, guests are never alone in the premises always family member here, everyone at risk during the night when asleep
Action taken to remove and reduce the hazards that may cause a fire	Chip pan replaced with deep fat fryer with thermostat Peroxides limited to one small bottle Interlinked smoke alarms with 10 year batteries fitted in bedrooms and landing on first floor and in lounge on ground floor
Action taken to remove and reduce the risk to people from a fire	All family members know the fire escape plan, and how to use the kitchen fire extinguisher. Information leaflet in all bedrooms showing escape route. Routine established of closing all doors at night and making sure everything turned off. 2 x ill-fitting doors replaced by solid timber doors

Assessment/review

Assessment/review date	Completed by	Signature

Appendix 3 – an example of an Access Statement

Access Statement

Rhubarb Cottage is situated in The Custards, a quiet cul de sac road which has no through traffic. The cottage is about 100 metres from the open forest on a level road. It is a 5 minute walk to Lyndhurst centre.

On arrival, a car can be parked in front of the cottage, parking parallel to the road with two wheels on the dedicated parking strip - this has a strengthened plastic lattice base which is covered in gravel.

The front door is 73 cms wide, 198 cms high and has a small step of 7cms.

The Entrance Hallway is 131 cms wide, with a minimum width of 100cms at the bottom of the stairs.

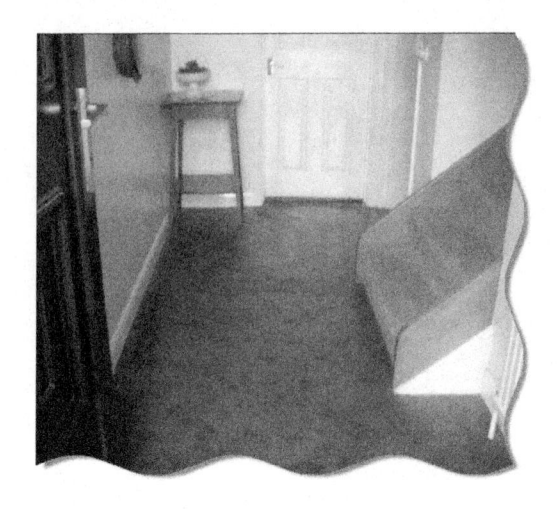

The cottage features a downstairs toilet off of the Hallway. The doorway is 64 cms wide and there is a wooden strip across the doorway, approx 1cm high.

All other doors in Rhubarb Cottage have a standard width of 70 cms.

> HOW TO SET UP AND RUN A SELF-CATERING
> HOLIDAY PROPERTY

The Hallway opens into the dining room which features an archway through to the lounge. There are no steps in this area.

The kitchen units are all of a standard height, with floor standing fridge and washing machine and eye level oven.

A 'Grab Handle' is fitted at the base of the stairs. The stairs themselves are 81 cms wide. They are not as steep as a standard set of stairs, making the cottage ideal for those who may find it difficult to climb steep stairs. There is a continuous wooden banister on one side of the stairs, from top to bottom.

On the first floor there are two bedrooms with double beds. There is access to both sides of the beds. All bed linen is non feather.

The bathroom features a bath with shower over. The bath is 57 cms high. There is a convenient Grab Handle at the end of the bath, to assist with climbing in and out.

There is one further bedroom on the second floor. This has two single beds and two velux window lights. Access to this bedroom is via another flight of stairs which is 66cms wide.

Access to the paved courtyard garden is via a wrought iron gate to the side of the cottage – 65cms wide. The back door leading out from the kitchen also opens onto the garden. There is a small step at the bottom of the door. Outside of the back door is a paved area of nine paving slabs with a small step down to the rest of the garden. Patio doors from the dining room also open out onto the garden via this step.

The garden itself is fully enclosed with wooden fencing panels.

Contact Information:

Rhubarb Cottage
The Custards
Lyndhurst
SO45 7AP
Tel: xxxxx xxxxxx
Email: info@escapetothenewforest.co.uk
www.escapetothenewforest.co.uk

HOW TO SET UP AND RUN A SELF-CATERING HOLIDAY PROPERTY

Appendix 4 – an example of a Landlord Gas Safety Certificate

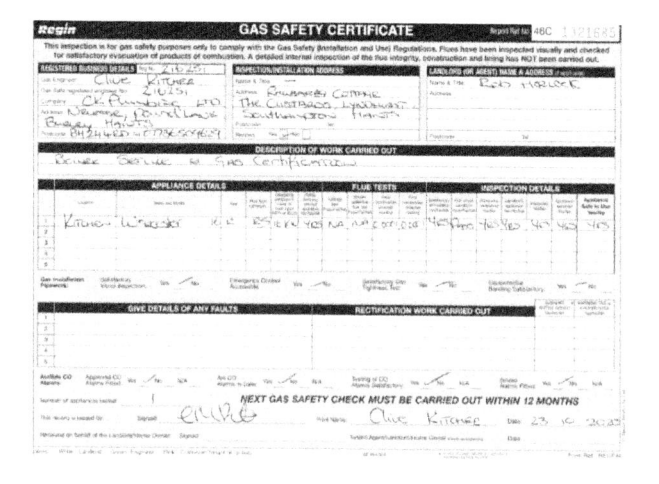

Appendix 5 – a suggested inventory for a Furnished Holiday Let

Kitchen

You should aim to provide two sets of plates, cups, saucers, mugs, glasses, cutlery, etc for your maximum occupancy. E.g if your maximum occupancy is 6, you should provide 12 of the above. This allows for items in the dishwasher (and breakages)

Apron
Baking trays
Bottle opener
Breadboard
Butter dish
Cafetiere
Cake tins
Can opener
Casserole dish
Champagne flutes
Chopping board
Colander
Cooking utensils
Corkscrew
Crockery
Cutlery
Draining rack
Egg cups
Fruit bowl
Glass bowls
Glasses – wine, tumblers (various)
Grater
Ice bucket
Ice cube tray

HOW TO SET UP AND RUN A SELF-CATERING HOLIDAY PROPERTY

Knife set (sharpened)
Masher
Measuring jug
Milk jug
Mortar and pestle
Mugs
Oven gloves
Placemats and coasters
Potato peeler
Roasting tins
Rolling pin
Rubbish bin
Saucepans (various)
Scissors
Serving bowls
Serving plates
Serving spoons
Sieve
Sink tidy
Spatula
Tea strainer
Tea towels
Tea, Coffee & Sugar (sachets?)
Teapot
Toast rack
Tray
Washing up bowl
Washing up liquid
Water Jug
Whisk
Wooden spoons

Bathroom
Bath mat
Hooks
Mirror
Non-slip shower mat
Soap dispenser/dish
Toilet brush
Toilet paper
Towels – small and large
Waste bin (lidded)

Bedrooms
Bedspreads
Bed linen
Blankets
Coat hangers
Duvets
Full-length mirror (near socket)
Hairdryers
Laundry basket
Make up mirror (illuminated)
Pillow protectors
Pillows
Travel cot
Waste bins
Waterproof mattress protectors

Electrical Equipment
Coffee machine
Dishwasher
DVD player
Fridge/Freezer
Hob
Iron

HOW TO SET UP AND RUN A SELF-CATERING HOLIDAY PROPERTY

Kettle
Microwave
Oven
Smart Speaker and/or Digital Radio
Smart TV
Toaster
USB charger
Vacuum cleaner
Washing machine/dryer
Wireless router for internet access

Safety

Carbon monoxide alarm
Fire blanket
Fire extinguisher
First aid kit
Plasters
Sewing kit
Smoke alarm
Wind-up torch

Other

Attractions leaflets
Batteries
Books
Clothes dryer (or washing line and pegs)
Dog bowl
Doormat
Guides to attractions and walks
Highchair
Ironing board
Light bulbs

Magazines
Outside chairs and loungers
Outside table
Puzzles
Stair gate
Tablecloth
Table mats and coasters
Travel cot

Appendix 6 – an example of a Booking Schedule

Appendix 7 – Example of Guests' Holiday Guide

The Good Guest Guide

to a

Happy Holiday

Welcome to Honeysuckle Cottage and thank you for choosing to stay here. We sincerely hope that you have a great holiday.
If you have any queries that are not answered in this guide, please do not hesitate to ask.

Contacts:
Honeysuckle Cottage is owned by -
Name
Address
Tel: xxxxx xxxxxx
Mobile: xxxxx xxxxxx

In the event that you need to contact us, please 'phone either of the numbers above. We live nearby, so traffic permitting, we can usually come over within a short time. If you read nothing else in this guide, please ensure that all members of your party read the next section – Safety and Security.

> **HOW TO SET UP AND RUN A SELF-CATERING HOLIDAY PROPERTY**

Can we please ask that you ensure that you vacate the cottage by 10am on the morning that you are due to depart.

When you leave, please lock the front door and leave the key in the key safe.

PARKING: Details later in this manual – PLEASE DO NOT park in Race Course View – the residents have complained ☹

Safety, Security and Parking

First, the serious page....
Safety
Honeysuckle Cottage has a number of safety features:

The doors to all of the bedrooms are fire doors. These should be kept closed. This is particularly important at night.

The door between the hall and the dining room is also a fire door

There are electric smoke alarms on each floor

In the kitchen, you will find a fire blanket and a fire extinguisher. Please read the instructions to ensure that you know what to do, in the unlikely event of an emergency

A First Aid Kit is in the sideboard

Security
All of the exterior doors close by lifting up the handle and turning the key. Please then remove the key (so that you don't leave it in the lock, go out, then can't get back in)

Downstairs, the fanlight windows open. Upstairs the main windows also open (except the bathroom)

Please ensure that all doors are locked and windows are closed when you are not in the house

At night, please also ensure that doors are locked and large windows are closed

IMPORTANT: When you lock the doors, PLEASE DO NOT leave the key in the door. If you find that you lock yourself out and the key is still in the lock inside the door we will have to call a locksmith – which will be very expensive for you!! (and yes, this has happened before.)

Parking
Details of where to park and where not to park...
Please don't block anyone in and please don't park in front of any gates!

Useful Telephone Numbers
Doctor: xxxxxxxxx
A&E: xxxxx General Hospital, *address* xxxxxxxx
Police: xxxxxxxxx
Fire Brigade: xxxxxxxx
Coastguard: xxxxxxxxx

> **HOW TO SET UP AND RUN A SELF-CATERING HOLIDAY PROPERTY**

NHS Direct: (Confidential health advice plus location of the nearest Dentist who will see 'holiday' patients)   xxxxxxxx
Pharmacy: *Address* xxxxxxx
National Gas Emergency Service: xxxxxxxxx
Water Company: xxxxxxxx
Environment Agency: 0800 807060
RSPCA: 0870 5555999
Post Office: *Address* xxxxxxxxxx
Cash Machine: *Location*
Local Museums and Attractions: xxxxxxxx
Traveline: 0870 6082608
The nearest Public Telephone Box and Post Box are situated at xxxxxxxxxx
Public Transport: The nearest Railway Station is in xxxxxxx
Buses run from xxxxxxxxx

Taxis:
List of taxi firms with contact numbers

The nearest VET will be found at: *address and phone number*

When you arrive

Parking

Parking details

The Neighbours
Please respect the neighbours who live in the surrounding houses.

Where is everything? (examples)

First Aid Kit – in the sideboard

Freezer - there is a full-sized freezer in the summerhouse. If you wish to use this, turn it on at the socket on the back wall

Iron and Ironing Board – under the stairs, in the cupboard

Hair Dryer – one in each bedroom

Books, DVDs and Games – in the small unit in the Dining Room

Instructions to appliances – in the small unit in the Dining Room

Broom – in the shed

Dustbin – next to the shed

The Dustbin is emptied on TUESDAYS. Please put black bags at the front of the house for collection

Washing Line – a retractable washing line is on the fence post next to the shed (see 'In The Garden' section below)

Clothes Pegs – in the shed

Keys – in a pot on the sideboard

> HOW TO SET UP AND RUN A SELF-CATERING
> HOLIDAY PROPERTY

Tablecloths – (can be used on the tables indoors or outdoors) in the sideboard

Towels – in the cupboard on the First Floor Landing

Clothes Drying rail – under the stairs

In the upstairs cupboard in the hall you will find:

Waterproof Sheet for a single bed
Fittings for the stair gate – the stair gate is behind the cupboard

How do things work?
TV:

The Television is tuned to pick up terrestrial channels plus all of the Freeview channels. These should not require any further tuning.

DVD:

To watch a DVD, open the tray using the button at the top of the smaller remote. Insert a disc, press the same button and the disc will begin to play

If this does not start automatically, press the AV button on the TV remote

Pure DAB Radio/Bluetooth:

The radio has 10 pre-tuned Digital channels. Please do not save other channels over those already saved. Instructions for using the radio and for streaming Bluetooth from your phone etc are on the sideboard.

Central Heating:

The central heating (and hot water) is set to come on three times a day – morning, lunchtime and evening. Please try to resist the temptation to adjust the settings...

The thermostat is in the hall – in the interests of the environment and the gas bill, please don't leave it turned up too high.

Velux windows in the Loft room:

Pull the handle forward one click to let air into the room

Pull forward again to open the window

Reverse the process to close the window

There is a black out blind at each window. When you pull these down to close them, please pull down from the centre of the metal strip at the bottom, otherwise the blind may come out of the side strips

Please do not tape towels to the windows....

Recycling:

Please use clear bags for cardboard, cans, plastic bottles (not the tops) and paper. Other waste should be placed in black or pink bags.

In the garden

Table and chairs will be found in the summerhouse. Where practical, please store these back in the summerhouse if rain is forecast

On the post next to the shed you will find a retractable washing line. This can be extended out towards the house where it can be attached to one of the hooks that you will see in the walls. Once extended, the line must be wound around the plastic 'pins' under the washing line housing. This fixes the line at the desired length and stops it from sagging

FEEDING THE BIRDS: Many of our guests like to feed the birds and we would encourage you to do this. However, please don't put bread down on the ground as we don't want to encourage rats. The best place to feed the birds is on the summerhouse roof and you can watch them from the kitchen or sitting in the garden. You can fill the feeders with nuts or seeds.

In season, Blue Tits nest in the nestbox on the end of the house and House Martins nest under the eaves of Rhubarb Cottage.

What do we need to do when we leave?

Please make sure that all windows and doors are securely locked and closed

Turn off all of the lights

Turn down the thermostat (we will turn it up before the next guests arrive)

Lock the Front Door and leave the key in the key safe

Have a safe journey home and come back and see us again!

Honeysuckle Cottage

The cottage was built between 1897 and 1907. We believe that it was actually built while Queen Victoria was still on the throne.
It was originally built for families who lived and worked in the Forest. The owners were granted the right to graze ponies, cattle and donkeys on the open Forest (known as "Commoners' Rights").
In the late 1970s, the cottage was modernised, and the downstairs cloakroom and hall were added.

Lyndhurst (your local town/area – some local information)

The quickest way to walk to the centre of Lyndhurst is up Clarence Road, turn right, then left at the main road. There is a wide range of shops, cafes, restaurants, pubs and antique shops. The New Forest Visitor Centre is situated at the bottom of the main town centre car park, on the opposite side of the High St.

The Antique Centre, on the corner by the traffic lights is worth browsing. It is full if cupboards which are rented out to different dealers, so there is a wide range of items for sale.

Prezzos is an Italian restaurant with a very pleasant courtyard at the back. This is reasonably priced and good value.

At the bottom of the High St, is a café called La Parisienne, which is well worth visiting for breakfast or lunch.
Several of the restaurants do 'takeaways'.

The Forage is a nice cafe/restaurant in the High St which uses locally sourced food.

The Fish and Chip shop is also excellent (in our opinion...) Most of the shops, restaurants and bars in Lyndhurst are owned by the people that you meet when you walk through the door.

If you walk up the hill from the traffic lights you will come upon the church – St Michael & All Angels - on the left hand side. Alice Liddell, Lewis Carroll's inspiration for Alice in 'Alice in Wonderland' is buried in the churchyard (hence the references to Alice in Wonderland that you will see around the town – the Mad Hatters Tea Rooms, The White Rabbit pub, for example).

The New Forest

The New Forest is a National Park and a haven for wildlife.

The main trunk roads in the forest are fenced off and subject to the national speed limits. This includes the road from the M27 to Lyndhurst.

All other roads in the forest are open and the animals can wander across the roads at any time. For this reason, the speed limit on all open forest roads is a maximum of 40mph where safe to do so.

The ponies and all other animals in the forest are all owned by someone, though the animals are free to go wherever they please. In practice, they remain within a radius of about 2 miles.

Please be aware that the ponies and donkeys may bite and they can certainly kick. Do not stand behind them and do not feed them!

PLEASE DO NOT DROP LITTER IN THE FOREST ....

Pubs and Restaurants nearby

Local pubs that you might consider visiting include The Fox and Hounds (High St), The Waterloo Arms (walking distance across the main road into Lyndhurst), The Trusty Servant at Minstead, The White Hart in Cadnam. All do excellent food.

Farther afield, The Royal Oak at Fritham does very good basic pub food and The Three Tuns in Romsey has a contemporary menu. Most pubs have gardens where you can take dogs but some of these don't allow dogs inside the pub.

There are many restaurants throughout the forest at all levels. At weekends and busy periods, you will need to book in advance.

Les Mirabelles in Nomansland is a very nice French restaurant – expensive, but worth it. Next door is the

Lamb, a local pub that does good hearty food. Both of these buildings overlook the Nomansland Cricket Green. Details of the many and varied attractions in the forest can be found at The New Forest Visitor Centre.

Pubs that allow dogs in to the bar (at the time of writing):

The White Hart at Cadnam allows dogs in the bar area - recommended.

You can also take your (well behaved) dog to The Empress of Blandings, on the road from Cadnam to Ower. Pub Grub at reasonable prices. The Green Dragon at Brook does good food and has a decent garden at the back. The Bell Inn at Brook (by the golf course) allows dogs in the bar – you will need to book. The Old House at Home, in Romsey also allows dogs.

More locally, The Waterloo Arms, The Crown and Stirrup and The Swan all allow dogs into the bar.

(We give you these restaurant and pub recommendations in good faith based on our personal experience. We cannot accept responsibility if the pubs have changed hands or are not as described above due to a change in circumstances – or chefs! If you find that something has changed or would like another recommendation added to this guide, please leave a note for us and we will add it in, for the benefit of future guests.)

Appendix 8 – an example of Log Burner Instructions

Instructions for using the Log Burner

The log burner will get very HOT, so when you need to open the door to add wood or coal, or move the air controls, please use the glove and tool provided.

Lighting the Fire

Open the door by lifting the handle (1) to the left.

HOW TO SET UP AND RUN A SELF-CATERING HOLIDAY PROPERTY

If the ash pan needs to be emptied, this can be emptied into a black bag only if the ash is cold. If the ash is warm or hot, use the Ash Bucket which you will find in the shed.

Put in a firelighter and light it.

Add a good handful of kindling, arranging it over and around the firelighter.

Shut the door and secure by turning the handle back down to face towards the floor.

Loosen the knob at the top of the door (2) and slide to the left to open the vent.

Loosen the knob at the bottom (3) and slide to the left as well. This ensures a good airflow through the fire to get the fire going.

When the kindling is burning well, open the door and add 1 or 2 logs - the door may be HOT by this time. If it is, use the glove.

Close the door.

When the logs start to burn and you think that the fire is going well, slide the top and bottom sliders over to the right, not quite all the way. This restricts the airflow and generates more heat. The knobs are likely to be HOT.

If the fire fails to catch, add more kindling.

You can use logs or coal in the fire. A mix of both generates the most heat.

Do not fill the whole fire with logs and coal. 2 Logs and a few lumps of coal are plenty. Top up when necessary.

Please remember that fire is extremely dangerous. NEVER leave the door open when the fire is burning

Appendix 9 - an example of setting up WIFI

HOW TO SET UP AND RUN A SELF-CATERING HOLIDAY PROPERTY

Using Broadband

Please note that in order to use broadband, you must have a wireless enabled laptop (or tablet, smartphone, etc). The broadband service is provided with 'best endeavours' and we cannot be liable if you are unable to connect to the internet due to specific security settings on your laptop.

Instructions

Ensure that the broadband unit is switched on and the telephone cable is plugged in (in the dining room, by the door to the hallway).

Switch on your device. It should detect all local wireless connections.

Select the Vodafone option which ends in xxx

The password is **jsjbtxx55nam89!**

This should enable you to access the internet.

When you have finished, please leave the broadband unit switched on.

Appendix 10 - an example of Terms & Conditions

Terms & Conditions – Rhubarb Cottage

1. Rhubarb Cottage is a self-catering holiday cottage in Lyndhurst and must be used as a private holiday residence for the occupation only of the persons specified on the booking form (The Hirers).
2. The number of persons occupying Rhubarb Cottage must not exceed six, for which beds and linen are provided. Any exceptions to this must be agreed with the owners at the time of booking.
3. The cottage should be left in a clean and tidy state on departure. The hirers will vacate it at the termination time and date without any prior warning or process of law.
4. The hirers' car(s) is parked outside of the cottage at the hirers' own risk and all personal possessions are left on the premises at the hirers' own risk.
5. No responsibility is accepted by the owners for any accidental mishap to persons or property whilst on the premises, or whilst engaged in any activity therefrom, or for any illness or injury arising from cause whatsoever.
6. The owners may cancel the booking if the cottage becomes unsuitable for occupation due to circumstances beyond their reasonable control, such as flood or fire damage. In such a situation a full refund will be made of all sums paid. The owners will have no further liability to the hirers.

HOW TO SET UP AND RUN A SELF-CATERING HOLIDAY PROPERTY

7. If, for any reason outside of the control of the owners, the cottage is not available to the hirers on the date of their confirmed booking, the owners will offer the hirer alternative dates, waiving any administration charges for the service. The hirer will not be entitled to any further claim from the owners.

8. Access by the owners may be required on occasions.

9. No smoking is permitted inside Rhubarb Cottage.

10. Under no circumstance may the hirers hold a party at or in Rhubarb Cottage.

11. A £75 damage deposit is payable. The damage deposit will be repaid within 7 working days, providing that the cottage and its contents are in the original state, as the hirers found it, at the commencement of their holiday. The hirers should notify the owners of any breakage or damage and re-imburse them prior to departure. The cost of any damages which have not been re-imbursed will be deducted from the damage deposit.

12. Any pets which are on holiday with their owners must be kept strictly under control. In particular, they must not be allowed on the furniture, including chairs and beds. The hirers will forfeit their £75 damage deposit, in full, if pets' hair is found on furniture, to cover the cost of the extra cleaning.

13. A 25% deposit is payable at the time of booking and the balance (plus the £75 damage deposit) is payable at least six weeks before commencement of the hire period. In the case of bookings within six weeks of the hire date, the full cost of the hire is payable at the time of booking.

14. Cancellation - If the hirers have to cancel the holiday, they must notify the owners immediately. The owners will attempt to re-let the property. Until the owners are able

to re-let the property for the period of the hire, all balances must be paid, as and when they become due. If the owners cannot re-let the cottage, the hirers will remain liable for the full cost of any part of the holiday that is not re-let. If the owners are able to re-let the hire period, they will refund to the hirers whatever the hirers have paid at that time, less an administration charge of 10% of the total value of the holiday.

A word of advice:

You are strongly recommended to take out Holiday Cancellation Insurance. To obtain a quotation, click on the following link:

moneysupermarket

Note: The owners of Rhubarb Cottage do not receive any payment whatsoever from any insurance policy which you may take out. However, it will be a sound investment for you, in the unlikely event of a holiday cancellation.

Making a booking of Rhubarb Cottage constitutes acceptance of these Terms and Conditions.

GDPR: Any information given by you at the time of booking is never used for any other purpose than your booking. This information is never shared with any other organisation.

======== THE END ========

HOW TO SET UP AND RUN A SELF-CATERING HOLIDAY PROPERTY

Other books by Rob:

Self Help:

LIFT – 99 Ways to LIFT your career

Children's series - Creature Teachers:

The Skylark Who Was Frightened of Flying

The Cat Who Wore a Hat

The Giraffe Who Couldn't Laugh

The Dog Who Watched TV

The Rabbit Who Hopped Over the Hill

Creature Teachers - the 5 books above in one set

Memories From the 20th Century:

How Was It for You? – memories of the 1940s

I Remember When I was Young – memories of the 1920s – 1960s

Humour:

Penguin Dave's 100 Really Funny Jokes

HOW TO SET UP AND RUN A SELF-CATERING HOLIDAY PROPERTY

YouTube:

Rob is also a Youtuber. His channel is 'The Country Traveller' and includes videos on Walks (virtual walks for exercise, narrated historic walks), Nature, The New Forest and Travel.

Please feel free to subscribe ...

Link: The Country Traveller

======== THE END ========

Printed in Great Britain
by Amazon